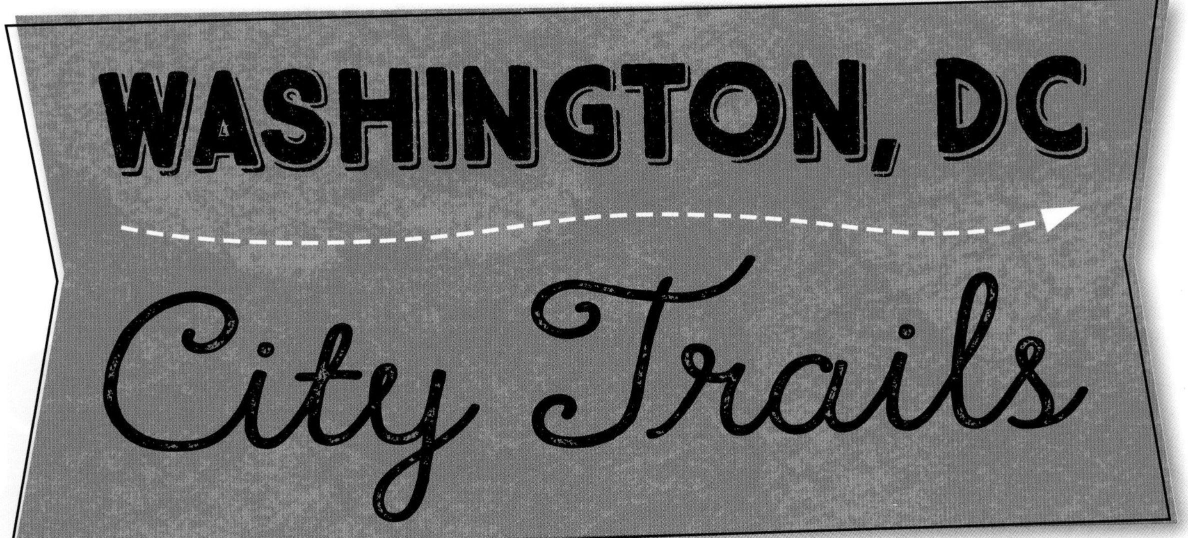

Moira Butterfield

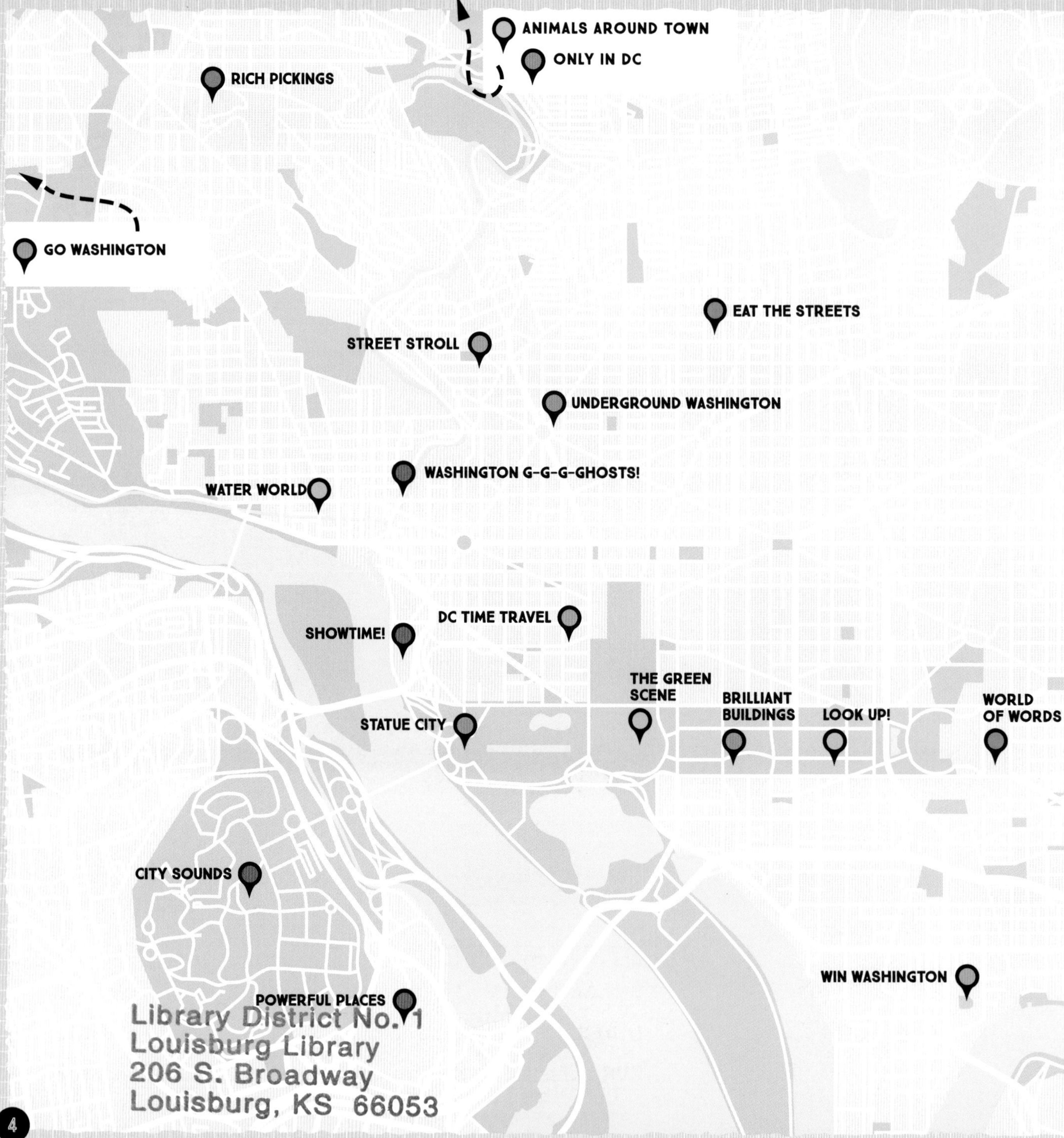
ANIMALS AROUND TOWN
ONLY IN DC
RICH PICKINGS
GO WASHINGTON
EAT THE STREETS
STREET STROLL
UNDERGROUND WASHINGTON
WASHINGTON G-G-G-GHOSTS!
WATER WORLD
DC TIME TRAVEL
SHOWTIME!
THE GREEN SCENE
BRILLIANT BUILDINGS
LOOK UP!
WORLD OF WORDS
STATUE CITY
CITY SOUNDS
WIN WASHINGTON
POWERFUL PLACES

Hi... we're Amelia and Marco, and we've created 19 awesome themed trails for you to follow.

The pushpins on this map mark the starting points, and each trail is packed with insider secrets and loads of cool stuff. So whether you are a culture vulture, a sports fanatic, or a history buff, this book has got something for you!

CONTENTS

PAGE NUMBER

DC TIME TRAVEL

Washington, DC, was founded in 1790 by George Washington, the first president of the US. It's seen over 200 years of important US history, so it's a great place to go time traveling. Are you ready to whizz back through some of Washington's history highlights? Let's travel through time!

MISTAKEN IDENTITY

OLD STONE HOUSE

The Old Stone House was built in 1765, before the city was even begun. It's the city's oldest building still in its original spot, and it's here today because it was preserved by mistake! When George Washington first planned the city, he had meetings with landowners in a local inn, and for years afterwards, the Old Stone House was mistakenly believed to be the historic meeting site. That was actually a location nearby, but the Old Stone House got the credit.

SIX-SIDED SAFETY

OCTAGON HOUSE

Washington was nearly destroyed soon after it was founded, when it was almost burned to the ground during the War of 1812 against the British. James Madison, the fourth US president, and his family had to get out fast when the White House was destroyed, and they ended up in the six-sided (so strangely named) Octagon House for a while. British troops only invaded the city for 24 hours but they managed to wreck a number of government buildings, including the Capitol and the Library of Congress.

INVADING BRITISH SOLDIERS PILED UP FURNITURE IN THE UNFINISHED CAPITOL BUILDING, ADDED SOME GUNPOWDER, AND LIT THE LOT! NEXT, THEY WENT TO THE WHITE HOUSE, WHERE THEY GRABBED FOOD AND DRINK, AND STOLE SOME SOUVENIRS, BEFORE SETTING FIRE TO THE BUILDING. THE WAR ENDED WITH A TREATY SIGNED BY JAMES MADISON IN THE OCTAGON HOUSE.

ESCAPE AT LAST

MOUNT ZION CEMETERY

Before the American Civil War (1861–1865), slavery was legal in the US. The people of the Mount Zion United Methodist Church – DC's oldest black congregation – hid escaping slaves in an old cemetery burial vault here in the 1800s. It was a stop on the Underground Railroad, a network of safe houses and escape routes that helped slaves escape to freedom. The city gave slaves their freedom in April 1862, nine months before it became a national law.

MOUNT ZION CEMETERY

FORT STEVENS

ACCORDING TO A DIARY OF THE BATTLE: "A SOLDIER ROUGHLY ORDERED HIM TO GET DOWN OR HE WOULD HAVE HIS HEAD KNOCKED OFF." THE CITY'S DEFENSES HELD UNTIL REINFORCEMENTS ARRIVED, BUT IT WAS A CLOSE CALL.

DUCK!

FORT STEVENS

Abraham Lincoln, the 16th president, led the Union forces from Washington during the Civil War between the Union (the North) and the Confederacy (the South). A short but fierce battle raged at this fort for two days between the 11th and 12th of July, 1864. Lincoln stood on a parapet to see the fighting and came under fire from Confederate sharpshooters.

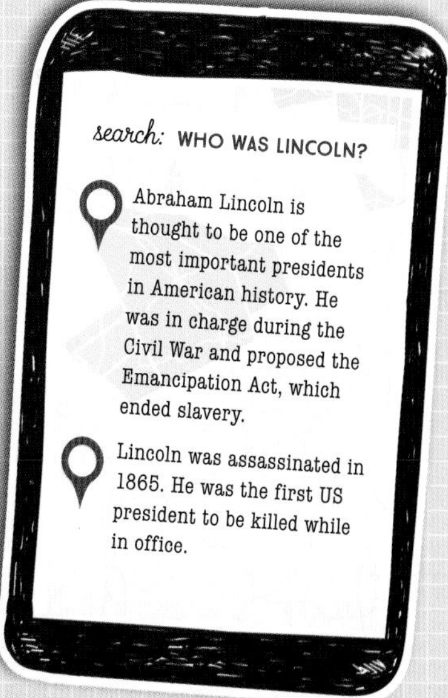

search: WHO WAS LINCOLN?
Abraham Lincoln is thought to be one of the most important presidents in American history. He was in charge during the Civil War and proposed the Emancipation Act, which ended slavery.
Lincoln was assassinated in 1865. He was the first US president to be killed while in office.

HISTORY'S HOUSE ON THE HILL

PRESIDENT LINCOLN'S COTTAGE

President Abraham Lincoln came to this hilltop house with his family in summer to escape the heat of the city. Here, he made some of the most important decisions in US history, directing the Civil War and planning his anti-slavery Emancipation Proclamation. He spent summers at the cottage between 1862 and 1865. He would ride from the cottage to the White House on horseback, past the military camps, slave refugee camps, and military defenses that were in the city during Civil War times.

ANACOSTIA PARK

LONG BEFORE DC

ANACOSTIA PARK

Native American people lived in the Washington area for thousands of years before Europeans first arrived in the 1600s. The village of Nacotchtank was the largest of the three Native American villages in the DC area. It was on the southeast side of the river, in the area between today's Bolling Air Force Base and Anacostia Park. The name Anacostia is a European version of the name Nacotchtank.

WHEN EUROPEANS CAME, THINGS CHANGED QUICKLY FOR THE NACOTCHTANK PEOPLE. THE FIRST TO ARRIVE WAS EXPLORER CAPTAIN JOHN SMITH IN 1608. HE MADE A MAP OF THE AREA, SHOWING NATIVE AMERICAN TOWNS. BY THE 1670S, THE LOCAL NATIVE AMERICANS HAD DIED FROM DISEASE, BEEN KILLED, OR DRIVEN AWAY.

THANK YOU, MR. SMITHSON

JAMES SMITHSON'S CRYPT

James Smithson was an eccentric British scientist. Even though he had never visited the US, Smithson had such a high regard for it that he left his fortune to the country to set up the Smithsonian Institution. He said he wanted his money to further knowledge, and that certainly happened. The Smithsonian now has 19 museums and galleries (a whopping 17 of them are in Washington), plus a zoo. Smithson died in 1929 and was buried in Italy, but 75 years later, he finally made the journey west when his body was brought to the US and reburied in the Smithsonian Castle on the National Mall. Visitors can see his crypt and thank him for themselves!

JAMES SMITHSON'S CRYPT

PEOPLE'S PARK

NATIONAL MALL

This world-famous park runs through the heart of Washington. It's home to 14 free museums, plus famous monuments and memorials, some of which you'll discover in other trails. It's come a long way from its early life as a wild and dangerous strip of marshy land where goats grazed.

ALL KINDS OF MARCHES AND RALLIES HAVE BEEN HELD ON THE NATIONAL MALL. ONE OF THE MOST FAMOUS WAS THE MARCH FOR AFRICAN AMERICAN RIGHTS LED BY MARTIN LUTHER KING JR. IN 1963. HE GAVE HIS FAMOUS "I HAVE A DREAM" SPEECH ON THE STEPS OF THE LINCOLN MEMORIAL.

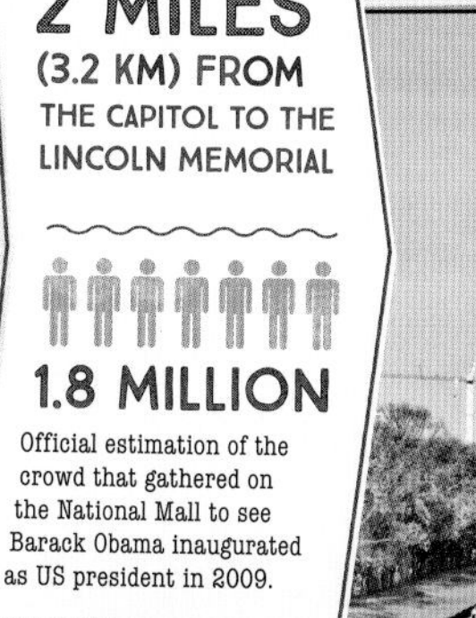

2 MILES
(3.2 KM) FROM THE CAPITOL TO THE LINCOLN MEMORIAL
1.8 MILLION
Official estimation of the crowd that gathered on the National Mall to see Barack Obama inaugurated as US president in 2009.

HISTORICAL ARTIFACTS

NATIONAL MUSEUM OF AMERICAN HISTORY

Thousands of objects from America's history are kept here, showing how the lives of Americans have changed over time. It's run by the Smithsonian Institution and it's free for everyone to see. Here are just a few of its historic highlights.

ABE LINCOLN'S HAT

President Abraham Lincoln was famous for wearing a battered-looking top hat called a stovepipe hat. He stored important papers under his hat when it was on his head! He was a tall man – the tallest president so far at 6 ft. 4 in. (1.93 m) – and the hat made him even taller, so he always stood out in a crowd. When he was assassinated in a theater (see page 47), the hat now on display in the museum was on the floor by his chair.

GEORGE WASHINGTON'S SWORD

George Washington wore this steel sword and scabbard during the Revolutionary War against Britain. He was an experienced fighter and an expert horseman who was used to surviving in the wilderness. When he died, he left five swords to five nephews, but told them they must only use them to defend themselves or their country and its rights.

MONEY MUSEUM

This museum is home to one of the biggest collections of coins, paper money, and medals in the world. It contains two examples of one of the most valuable coins in the world – a 1933 double eagle $20 gold piece. Each one is worth $7.6 million.

DOROTHY'S MAGIC SHOES

HAVE YOU EVER SEEN THE FAMOUS OLD MOVIE *THE WIZARD OF OZ*? ACTRESS JUDY GARLAND PLAYED THE PART OF DOROTHY, A LITTLE GIRL WHO TRAVELS TO THE LAND OF OZ. SHE WEARS A PAIR OF MAGICAL RUBY SLIPPERS THAT TAKE HER HOME WHEN SHE CLICKS HER HEELS. THE RUBY RED SHOES FROM THE FILM ARE IN THE MUSEUM, ALONG WITH MANY OTHER FAMOUS OBJECTS FROM STAGE AND SCREEN.

THE STAR-SPANGLED ORIGINAL

On the morning of September 14, 1812, soldiers raised a US flag over Fort McHenry in Baltimore to celebrate surviving a bombardment by British ships. An American lawyer called Francis Scott Key was watching from a US ship and was so stirred by the sight of the flag he wrote a song – "The Star-Spangled Banner" – which eventually became the national anthem of the US. The original flag is on display in its own environmentally controlled chamber.

30,000+
PIECES OF CLOTHING AND ACCESSORIES IN THE MUSEUM

4,000
NUMBER OF AMERICAN TOYS IN THE MUSEUM

CITY SOUNDS

Tiptoe along our special city sound trail and listen carefully to discover some sounds that will remind you of the nation's capital.

ARLINGTON CEMETERY

TAPS TRUMPETS

ARLINGTON NATIONAL CEMETERY

This huge military cemetery is the final resting place of over 400,000 members of the US military and their families, from every conflict in the country's history. When funerals and memorial events are held here, a bugle plays a melody called *Taps*. The 24 solemn notes of *Taps* are played around 30 times a day.

TAPS WAS FIRST PLAYED AROUND 150 YEARS AGO DURING THE CIVIL WAR, AS A SIGNAL FOR UNION SOLDIERS TO PUT OUT THEIR CAMPFIRES AT NIGHT.

SKY CELEBRATION

INDEPENDENCE DAY FIREWORKS

Every year on July 4, Independence Day is celebrated on the National Mall with a spectacular fireworks display set to music. In total, around 6,500 fireworks blast off during a super-noisy 17.5 minutes. The rockets shoot up 1,500 ft. (457 m) into the sky, controlled by fireworks experts via a computer at the Lincoln Memorial.

NATIONAL MALL

PRESIDENTS, VICE PRESIDENTS, AND THEIR FAMILIES HAVE BEEN PRESSING THE BUTTON TO LIGHT THE NATIONAL CHRISTMAS TREE SINCE 1923. PRESIDENT HARRY TRUMAN USED TO SWITCH ON THE LIGHTS REMOTELY FROM HIS VACATION HOME IN MISSOURI.

HAPPY HOLIDAYS

CHRISTMAS CHOIRS AROUND THE NATIONAL XMAS TREE

Every Christmas, the National Christmas Tree is decorated on the grounds of the Ellipse, a park area south of the White House. A stage is added, too, and big-name stars perform carols with a military band on the night of the tree lighting on December 1. Then, there is nightly choir music around the tree for two weeks.

WHITE HOUSE

NATIONAL MUSEUM OF AFRICAN AMERICAN HISTORY AND CULTURE

OLD SATCHMO

LOUIS ARMSTRONG'S TRUMPET

Louis Armstrong (nicknamed "Satchmo") was one of the greatest jazz trumpeters of all time, and his trumpet is treasured at Washington's National Museum of African American History and Culture. It was custom-made for him in Paris in 1946, but it still sounds good according to fellow trumpet maestro Wynton Marsalis, who was allowed to play it in 2015. It was a rare honor, and Marsalis said he was extra-careful.

GO-GO TOWN

CHUCK BROWN MEMORIAL

Washington has its very own funky dance music style called go-go, invented in the 1970s by the godfather of go-go, Chuck Brown. In the 1980s, the city was full of go-go bands, and the style influenced dance music in other parts of the US. Northeast DC's Langdon Park is home to a musical memorial to Chuck Brown, with added toy instruments and drums for visitors to play. It's on a patch of grass shaped like a giant guitar pick.

7 TONS (6,350 KG)

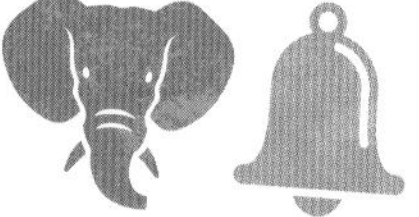

Weight of the largest Taft Memorial bell, (the bourdon) = roughly the weight of an adult male African elephant.

FOR A TASTE OF WASHINGTON GO-GO MUSIC, GO ONLINE TO CHECK OUT CHUCK BROWN'S BIGGEST HIT – "BUSTIN' LOOSE."

BIG BELLS

TAFT MEMORIAL CARILLON

A marble tower 100 ft. (30.5 m) high stands on the grounds of the Capitol building. It's fitted with a musical instrument called a carillon, a line of bells that chime together automatically to play music on the hour and every quarter-hour. At 2 p.m. on July 4, the 27 tower bells are played by hand by the official carillonneur (bell ringer) of Capitol Hill. They ring out "The Star-Spangled Banner" and "America the Beautiful."

MERIDIAN HILL PARK

DRUM DAY

MERIDIAN HILL PARK (OR MALCOLM X PARK)

Every Sunday afternoon since the 1950s, there's been a drum circle in the park. Drum enthusiasts arrive to beat out a rhythm, and they're often joined by dancers, tightrope walkers, jugglers, hula-hoopers, and families grooving along to the city's weekly beat.

search: DC MUSIC MAKERS

MARVIN GAYE

This famous Motown singer was born in Washington in 1939.

DUKE ELLINGTON

Born in DC in 1899, Edward Ellington was given the nickname "Duke" and went on to become one of the best-known jazz musicians of the 20th century. You can read more about him on page 99.

U STREET

DREAM STREET

FUNK PARADE

The U Street neighborhood of Washington was once well known for its parades, but they had died out until local resident Justin Rood had a vivid dream one night. He dreamt he saw bands marching along and playing, and when he woke up, he decided to make it happen for real! In 2014, he and his neighbors started the Funk Parade, a street festival that celebrates the area's music with a parade of lively dancers and bands.

STATUE CITY

Washington is dotted with outdoor statues and sculptures of all sorts, from famous leaders to space villains and giant spiders. Step this way for some statue surprises.

HOW DOES LINCOLN LOOK?

The sculptor Daniel Chester French used 28 blocks of marble to make Lincoln's likeness, and spent years studying the man so the statue would properly represent his character. Some people think that Abe looks sad, some think he looks thoughtful, and others believe that his expression changes depending on the angle you look from. What do you think?

THE BIG MAN

LINCOLN MEMORIAL

More people visit the Lincoln Memorial than any other memorial in DC. It's designed to look like an Ancient Greek temple, with Abraham Lincoln sitting inside. It has been the location of many marches and rallies (see page 7).

LINCOLN MEMORIAL

MARBLE MESSAGES

Henry Bacon, the architect, wanted the memorial of the man who abolished slavery and defended democracy to echo the Parthenon in Ancient Greece, where democracy was first born. The memorial has three chambers – one for Lincoln's statue and two for wall carvings of his speeches along with mural paintings of his ideas and achievements.

LINCOLN'S STATUE
19 FT.
(5.79 M) HIGH

36 COLUMNS
Symbolize the number of states in the Union at the time of Lincoln's death.

48 INSCRIPTIONS
One for each of the states at the time the memorial was completed in 1922. Alaska and Hawaii became states later. They share a special commemorative plaque.

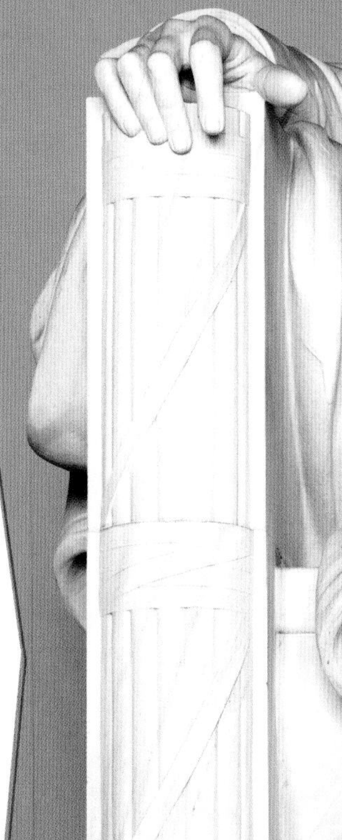

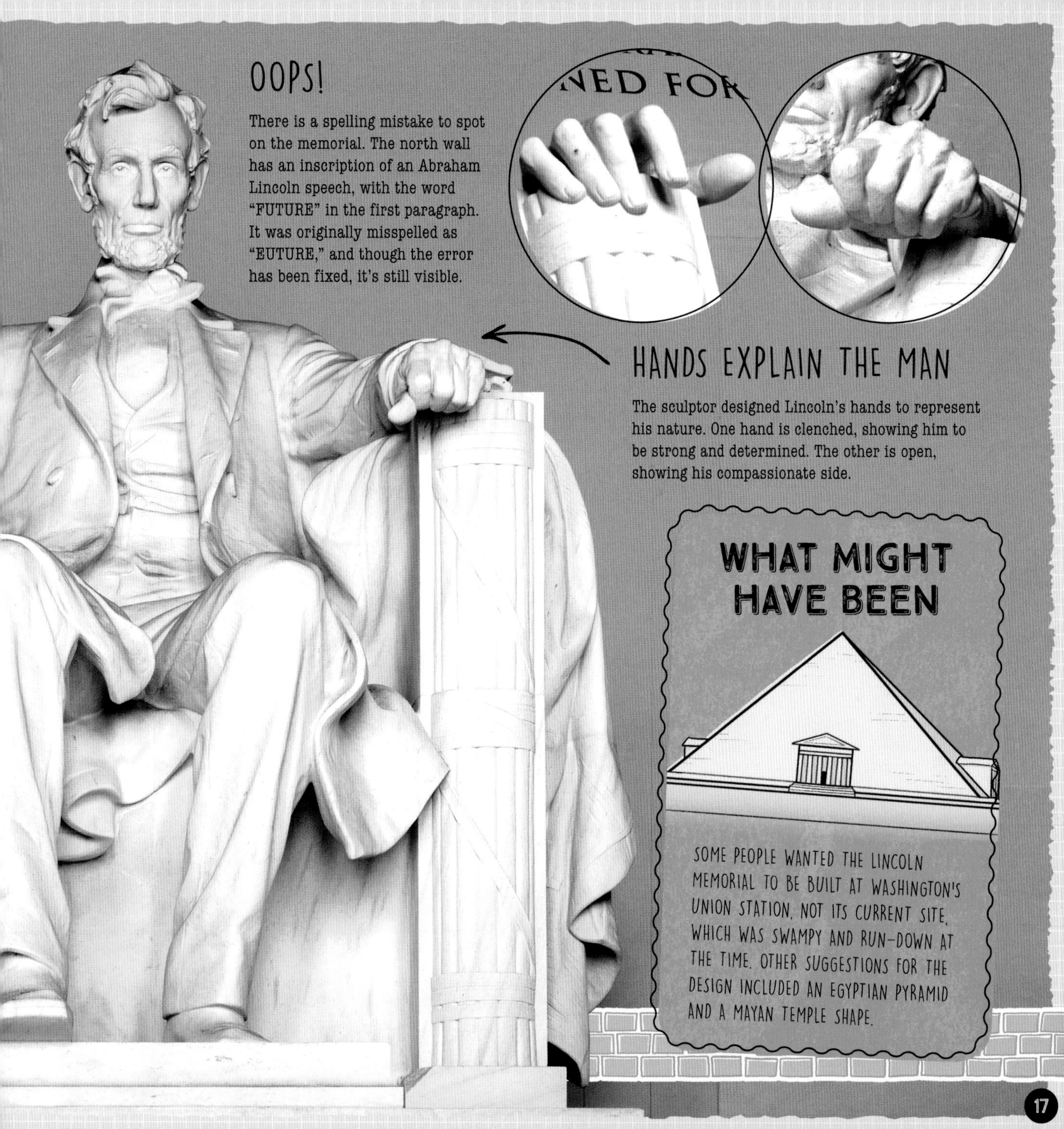

OOPS!

There is a spelling mistake to spot on the memorial. The north wall has an inscription of an Abraham Lincoln speech, with the word "FUTURE" in the first paragraph. It was originally misspelled as "EUTURE," and though the error has been fixed, it's still visible.

HANDS EXPLAIN THE MAN

The sculptor designed Lincoln's hands to represent his nature. One hand is clenched, showing him to be strong and determined. The other is open, showing his compassionate side.

WHAT MIGHT HAVE BEEN

SOME PEOPLE WANTED THE LINCOLN MEMORIAL TO BE BUILT AT WASHINGTON'S UNION STATION, NOT ITS CURRENT SITE, WHICH WAS SWAMPY AND RUN-DOWN AT THE TIME. OTHER SUGGESTIONS FOR THE DESIGN INCLUDED AN EGYPTIAN PYRAMID AND A MAYAN TEMPLE SHAPE.

WITHIN THE ROOMS OF THE BIG MEMORIAL THERE'S A LINE OF LIFE-SIZED BRONZE PEOPLE IN A BREADLINE DURING THE GREAT DEPRESSION, PLUS STATUES OF THE PRESIDENT, HIS WIFE, ELEANOR ROOSEVELT, AND HIS FAITHFUL FIRST DOG, FALA.

REMEMBERED TWICE

FRANKLIN D. ROOSEVELT MEMORIALS

Roosevelt was the longest-serving president in US history, and he has two memorials in town. His big memorial has four open rooms that tell the story of his time in office, from the Great Depression to World War II. But Roosevelt himself only wanted a modest stone slab the size of his desk, which is by the National Archives building. Congress granted his wish but later decided to build the biggie on the Mall.

WORLD WAR II MEMORIAL

A SOLDIER'S MARK

NATIONAL WORLD WAR II MEMORIAL

The World War II Memorial is a beautiful way to remember the soldiers who took part in the conflict, but it also has a hidden secret. During World War II, US soldiers liked to draw a popular graffiti character wherever they went. It was a picture of a big-nosed man peeking over a wall under the words "Kilroy was here." Kilroy has even managed to sneak onto the World War II Memorial. After a row of columns representing the states, there's an alcove with his picture engraved on the wall. He's hiding in an alcove on the other side of the memorial, too.

SEEING KILROY ON A WALL WAS A COMFORT TO US SOLDIERS FIGHTING AWAY FROM HOME DURING THE WAR. HIS PICTURE WAS A SIGN THAT OTHER AMERICAN TROOPS HAD BEEN THERE.

WASHINGTON MONUMENT

FIND THE COLOR CLUE

WASHINGTON MONUMENT

This column, honoring George Washington, is the tallest structure in DC. When it was completed, it was the world's tallest building and it's still the tallest stone obelisk on the planet. It took so many years to build that the marble used had to come from different quarries, and there's a clue for eagle-eyed stone spotters...

555 FT. (169 M) HIGH

ABOUT 150 FT. (46 M) UP, THE COLOR CHANGES AT THE PLACE WHERE THE DIFFERENT STONES MEET.

897

NUMBER OF STEPS INSIDE MONUMENT

Luckily, there's an elevator for the public to use. It was once steam-powered.

NATIONAL GALLERY

MAGIC ON THE MALL

NATIONAL GALLERY SCULPTURE GARDEN

This National Mall location is known for modern art sculptures, and its display includes a giant spider, a giant row of stacked floating chairs, a moon-dog, and a house that grows bigger or smaller. *The Spider*, by Louise Bourgeois, partly represents her own mom – a powerful protector but also delicate. Nearby *House 1*, by Roy Lichtenstein, is a clever optical illusion. As you walk past, it seems to change size.

STATE BY STATE

NATIONAL STATUARY COLLECTION

There are 100 statues in the Capitol building, representing two famous citizens from each state. Originally, the statues were meant to stand together in the Statuary Hall but it got too crowded, so now there are 35 in the hall, and others are dotted round the building. Hawaii's statue of King Kamehameha I is the largest, weighing around 15,000 lb. (6,804 kg). He stands welcoming people to the visitor center.

CAPITOL BUILDING

WASHINGTON NATIONAL CATHEDRAL

LUKE, I'M UP HERE

WASHINGTON NATIONAL CATHEDRAL

In the 1980s, the Washington National Cathedral held a design competition for children to add some carvings to its towers. One of the winners submitted *Star Wars* villain Darth Vader, who is now high up on the cathedral along with a raccoon, a girl with braids and braces, and a man with large teeth carrying an umbrella.

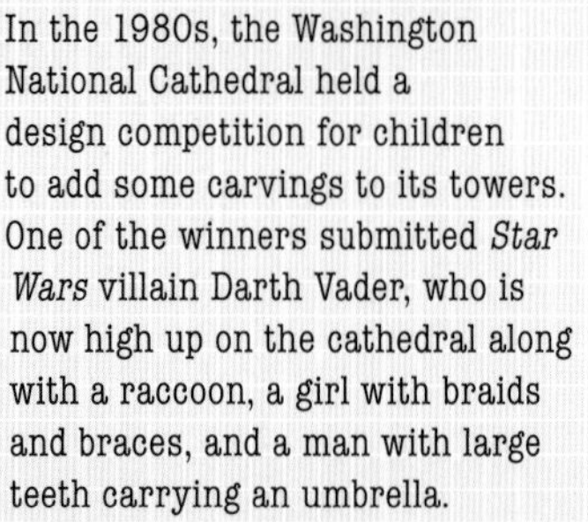

search: CAPITOL SOUNDS

EAVESDROP

An acoustic quirk caused by the Statuary Hall's half-dome shape means that a person standing in a particular place can clearly hear what someone is saying from all the way across the room, even if they're whispering.

MEET A GENIUS

ALBERT EINSTEIN MEMORIAL

Anyone can sit next to the world's most famous scientific genius on his bench outside the National Academy of Sciences. His bronze statue, by sculptor Robert Berks, relaxes next to an enormous star map. Over 2,700 metal studs mark the position of the sun, moon, planets, and stars at the exact time the statue was dedicated on April 22, 1979.

MOVIE MOMENT

WOMEN'S TITANIC MEMORIAL

If you've ever seen the movie blockbuster *Titanic*, you'll know the part where actress Kate Winslet poses with her arms out at the front of the doomed ship, which sank in 1912. She copied the pose from the Women's Titanic Memorial statue of a man who has been holding his arms out since 1931. It was paid for by a group of women (hence the name) who wanted to celebrate the heroes who gave their lives and commemorates the men who stood aside to let women and children go first to the lifeboats.

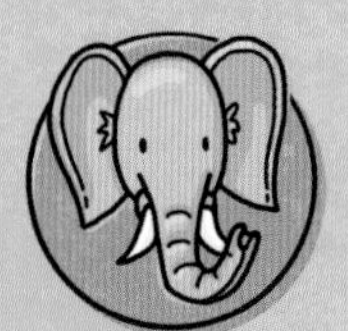

ANIMALS AROUND TOWN

Washington is home to around 670,000 people, but it's home to lots of animals, too. Follow the creature-spotting trail through the city to meet some of DC's creatures large and small, old and new.

NATURAL NEIGHBORS

ROCK CREEK PARK

There's something howling in town! Coyotes have moved into Rock Creek Park, a large area of woods, trails, and picnic spots not far from the heart of DC. They arrived around 2004, and they've turned up in other US cities, too. Nobody knows for sure how many there are in the park, but the National Park Service thinks they do a good job of keeping squirrel and mice numbers down.

HAPPY SWINGERS

NATIONAL ZOO

The National Zoo cares for many animals, but none are as high-flying as its orangutans. They have their own 50 ft. (15 m) high sky trail of steel cables and interconnecting towers, so they can swing between enclosures. It's nicknamed the O Line.

THE ZOO IS ALSO HOME TO SOME GIANT PANDAS. YOU CAN SEE WHAT THEY GET UP TO WHEREVER YOU ARE IN THE WORLD, THANKS TO THE TWO PANDA CAMS THAT BROADCAST THEIR EVERY MOVE ON THE ZOO'S WEBSITE.

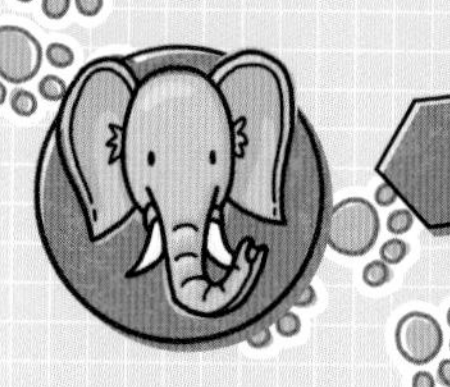

NATIONAL ZOO

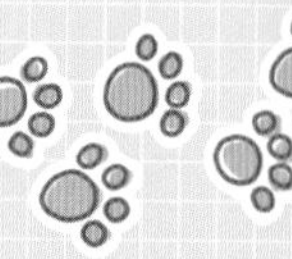

HIPPOPOTA'MISTAKE!

GEORGE WASHINGTON UNIVERSITY HIPPO

A bronze hippopotamus statue stands in front of the university's Lisner Auditorium, a gift from students in 2000. The plaque in front of it explains that years ago, hippos lived in the Potomac River near George Washington's home at Mount Vernon, and children used to lure them to shore and rub their noses for good luck. It's not true, but the legend lives on, and people still rub the hippo statue's nose for luck, especially at exam time.

WASHINGTON DID ONCE MENTION SEEING A HIPPO IN THE POTOMAC. HE WAS PROBABLY DESCRIBING A DREDGING MACHINE, BUT THE STUDENTS DECIDED TO TAKE HIM LITERALLY!

WHITE HOUSE GONE WILD

PRESIDENTIAL PETS

Many presidents have kept pets at the White House. William Howard Taft had a cow named Pauline. Woodrow Wilson kept a herd of sheep. Calvin Coolidge had a zoo-full, including Enoch the goose, Ebenezer the donkey, a bobcat, lion cubs, a bear, and a pygmy hippo called Billy. Theodore Roosevelt's family had around 40 animals, including a badger called Josiah, a hen called Baron Spreckle, a rabbit called Peter, a pig called Maude, and a snake called Emily Spinach.

CREATURE COMFORTS

NATIONAL MUSEUM OF NATURAL HISTORY

Hungry, hairy spiders, a cursed diamond, some ancient mummies, a sea monster, and two mysterious giant heads are among the exhibits waiting for visitors to this Smithsonian museum. No wonder it's one of the most popular visitor spots in town.

HELLO HENRY

Henry the African elephant greets visitors in the museum's atrium. He's 13 ft. (3.9 m) tall, and he was killed decades ago by hunters in Angola. He arrived at the zoo in 1959 and now helps teach visitors about elephant conservation and the banned ivory poaching trade. You can see what real African elephants are doing in the nearby National Zoo, via the museum's elephant cam.

MEET THE SPIDERS

Lots of insects and arachnids (spiders) live in the museum's Insect Hall, and volunteers sometimes bring out the tarantula spiders to meet visitors. Their venom isn't powerful. It feels rather like a bee sting to humans, and the spiders won't bite unless they are threatened with danger. Live crickets aren't so lucky. They become snacks for the tarantulas to eat at feeding time!

MOVIE STAR STONES

TWO STONE HEADS FROM RAPA NUI (EASTER ISLAND) LIVE IN THE MUSEUM. THEY WERE CARVED ON THE ISLAND FROM VOLCANIC TUFF – SOLIDIFIED ASH FROM AN EXTINCT VOLCANO. CARVINGS OF THIS KIND ARE CALLED *MOAI* AND THEY MAY REPRESENT THE HEADS OF TRIBAL ANCESTORS, BUT NOBODY KNOWS FOR SURE. IF YOU'VE SEEN THE *NIGHT AT THE MUSEUM* FILMS YOU'LL RECOGNIZE ONE OF THEM, ALONG WITH LOTS OF OTHER EXHIBITS IN THE MUSEUM.

126 MILLION+
SCIENCE SPECIMENS & CULTURAL ARTIFACTS

30 MILLION
INSECT SPECIMENS

4.5 MILLION
PLANT SPECIMENS

7 MILLION
FISH SPECIMENS

BLUE SPARKLER

An incredibly rare violet-colored diamond sits in a high-security display at the museum. It's called the Hope Diamond, and it comes from a mine in India. It once belonged to the doomed French Queen Marie Antoinette, who was executed in 1793. It's been sold to pay off debts and even stolen during its life, which has led some to say it's cursed. It's now part of a beautiful necklace set with 61 white diamonds.

ANIMALS UNDER WRAPS

You probably know that the Ancient Egyptians mummified dead humans, but they also mummified animals, including cats, birds, snakes, and even bulls. Some of these mummy creatures are on display at the museum. The Ancient Egyptians mummified their dead pets, but they also sacrificed animals to please the ancient Egyptian gods.

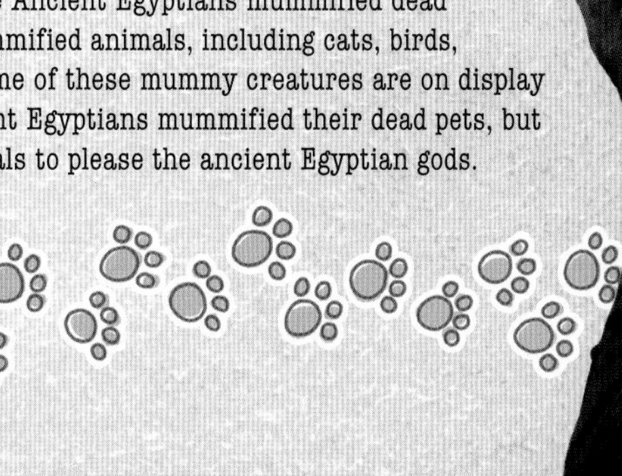

WAGGING AROUND THE WORLD

OWNEY THE STUFFED DOG

Owney was a scruffy stray terrier who became the unofficial mascot of the Railway Mail Service in the late 1800s, when the mail traveled around the US by train. He was seen as a good luck charm and was given medals and collar tags, collecting 1,017 tags in his lifetime. He even did a world tour. After he died, he was stuffed, and now sits wearing several of his tags in the Smithsonian's National Postal Museum. He has needed a bit of attention over the years, though, and has been patched up with a rabbit's foot and a pig's ear.

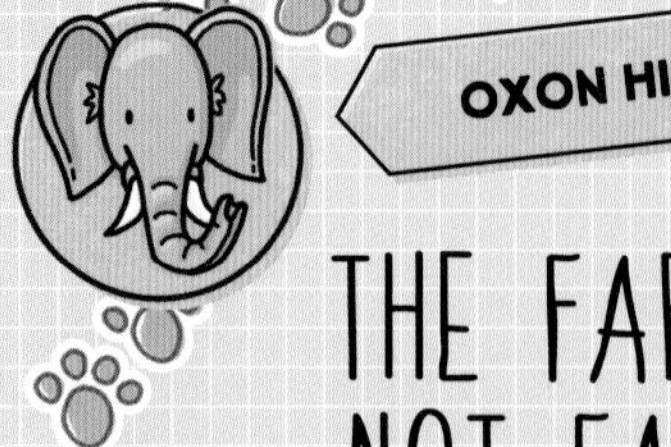

(140,000 MILES)
(225,308 KM)

DISTANCE OWNEY TRAVELED DURING HIS LIFETIME AS A MAIL MASCOT

THE FARM'S NOT FAR

OXON HILL FARM

Not far from the center of Washington is an old-fashioned farm, with an old barn, a tractor or two, and a cow called Duchess. Oxon Hill Farm is in Maryland, about 11 miles (18 km) south of the National Mall. City kids can go there to help milk the cows and feed the chickens. Cows, rabbits, chickens, pigs, goats, and horses live on the farm, which is now part of the National Park Service.

ANACOSTIA OASIS

KINGMAN ISLAND

This island oasis in the Anacostia River is home to more than 100 bird species, including ospreys, bald eagles, egrets, and blue herons. It was created from mud dredged up from the river in 1916. It's reached via a walkway, and as well as the birds, visitors might see turtles, beavers, and all sorts of insects.

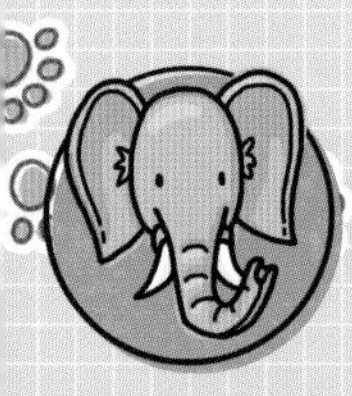

KINGMAN ISLAND

search: FAMOUS BIRDS OF WASHINGTON, DC

WOOD THRUSH

Back in 1938, this songbird was adopted as DC's official bird. Sadly, its numbers are now dropping.

DOVE OF PEACE

Just south of Washington, you can find a dove weather vane at the very top of Mount Vernon, George Washington's mansion.

BLESS THOSE PETS

FRANCISCAN MONASTERY AND NATIONAL CATHEDRAL

The Catholic feast day of St. Francis of Assisi, patron saint of animals, is on October 4. On the Sunday closest to that day, Washington pet owners can take their pets to be blessed at these two locations. Catholic priests sprinkle the animals with holy water, and they get to hear a service.

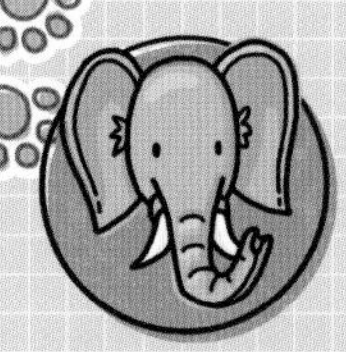

NATIONAL CATHEDRAL

WORLD OF WORDS

Washington is full of words that provide clues to its history. They will even help you find your way around. Follow the Washington word trail to learn about some of its letter-based locations.

LIBRARY OF CONGRESS

BOOKS, BOOKS, BOOKS

LIBRARY OF CONGRESS

The Library of Congress is the largest library in the world, with more than 162 million items on nearly 838 miles (1,349 km) of bookshelves. The British burnt down the library during the War of 1812 (see page 6), but President Thomas Jefferson sold over 6,000 of his own books to Congress to help it get up and running again. It adds around 12,000 new items to its collection every single day.

START

THE BARD'S BOOKS

FOLGER SHAKESPEARE LIBRARY

William Shakespeare, the world's most famous playwright, lived in England in the late 1500s. This library holds the largest collection of his works in the world, including editions of the *First Folio*, the earliest collection of his plays ever published. There were around 750 copies made. Only 233 copies survive, and the library has 82 of them. They're worth around $5 million each.

FOLGER SHAKESPEARE LIBRARY

THERE'S A PICTURE OF SHAKESPEARE AT THE FRONT OF EACH *FIRST FOLIO*. IT'S ONE OF ONLY TWO IMAGES OF THE BARD THAT EXIST. HE'S BALDING, WITH LONG HAIR AT THE SIDES AND A LITTLE HIPSTER MUSTACHE.

POWER OF THE WORDSMITH

FREDERICK DOUGLASS HOUSE

Frederick Douglass was an escaped slave who used the power of the word to argue for the end of slavery, and for the rights of all. He lived in this hilltop house from 1878 until his death in 1895, and he wrote books in the library here. His autobiography describing his life as a slave was published in 1845 and became a bestseller across the world, helping to influence how people felt about slavery.

FREDERICK DOUGLASS WAS A FRIEND OF PRESIDENT ABRAHAM LINCOLN, AND AFTER LINCOLN'S DEATH, MRS. LINCOLN SENT DOUGLASS HER LATE HUSBAND'S WALKING CANE, AS A SIGN OF THEIR FRIENDSHIP. IT'S ON DISPLAY IN HIS HOUSE.

FREDERICK DOUGLASS HOUSE

AVENUE CITY

CITY STREET NAMES

The city has roads named after each of the 50 American states. They're all avenues, with two exceptions – California Street and Ohio Drive. Pennsylvania Avenue is the address of the White House, and Massachusetts Avenue is the longest. Every year, a local cycling group rides down all 50 state-named roads – 62 miles (99.7 km) in total.

The city is divided into four quadrants (quarters) radiating out from the Capitol. The initials of the quadrants are used on street names. NW (Northwest), etc.

W ST NW

North or south of the Capitol building, the streets have letters of the alphabet, such as W Street.

14 ST NW

East or west, the streets are named with numbers, such as 14th Street NW.

Further out, they have alphabetically ordered words. First, there are two-syllable names (Belmont Street NW, for instance), then three-syllable names (Quackenbos Street NW, for instance). Far to the north of the city, the streets are named after flowers and trees (Butternut Street NW, for instance).

BELMONT ST NW

THE WATER'S ANCIENT NAME

POTOMAC RIVER

Washington, DC, is built on the banks of the Potomac River. The river's name comes from the word "Patawomeck," which is a Native American word meaning great trading place or place where people trade. The river would have made a good waterway for canoes and rafts bringing goods to and from other tribes. It flows along the city's west side, and the Anacostia River is on DC's east side.

POTOMAC RIVER

JEFFERSON MEMORIAL

"We hold these truths to be self-evident, that all men are created equal"
from the Declaration of Independence.

"God who gave us life gave us liberty"
from a letter to George Washington.

AMERICA'S FOUNDING WRITER

JEFFERSON MEMORIAL

There are lots of inscriptions around the memorial to Thomas Jefferson, third president of the US and author of the Declaration of Independence. They echo his writings and beliefs. Jefferson is said to be looking in the direction of another statue – that of his great political rival Alexander Hamilton. George Washington tried to bring the two men together, and his monument is between the two statues.

VIETNAM VETERANS MEMORIAL

SOLDIERS' SYMBOLS

VIETNAM VETERANS MEMORIAL

The black granite wall on the Mall is carved with 58,280 names of soldiers who died in the Vietnam War (1954–1975). A diamond symbol next to a name means that the soldier's death has been confirmed. A cross sign means the soldier is missing and unaccounted for. If a soldier ever returned alive, a circle would be inscribed around the cross sign – but as of yet, there are no circles on the wall.

FOGGY BOTTOM

search: INSIDER TALK

- What does it mean when somebody in Washington says "Inside the Beltway"? They're talking about the inner suburbs inside Interstate 495, called the Capital Beltway.
- Locals can have their own names for all kinds of things. In DC they refer to the Washington Monument as the "Pencil."
- American presidents have all been given nicknames, including "Little Jemmy," the name given to James Madison, the shortest president to date.

WHAT'S IN A NAME?

FOGGY BOTTOM

This strange neighborhood name comes from the smoke and fog that once used to hover over it when it was the low, damp location for lots of industrial workshops and factories. It was once home to lime kilns, glassworks, breweries, and gas companies, along with the poor immigrants who worked there. Now, it's an area of super-smart homes, George Washington University, and the US State Department.

THE NATION'S MOST IMPORTANT WORDS

NATIONAL ARCHIVES

The National Archives store official documents and records of all sorts. The US's three most iconic documents are kept here. First up is the Declaration of Independence (1776), then the Constitution (1787), and the Bill of Rights (1789). Together, these documents are called the Charters of Freedom, and they put into words the governing principles of the new nation.

10 BILLION APPROX. NUMBER OF TEXT PAGES

12 MILLION MAPS, CHARTS, ARCHITECTURAL AND ENGINEERING DRAWINGS

300,000 REELS OF MOTION PICTURE FILM

400,000 VIDEO AND SOUND RECORDINGS

NATIONAL ARCHIVES

INKED-IN INDEPENDENCE

The Declaration of Independence sets out the principles of the new country, independent from Britain. It was signed on August 2, 1776, by 56 people, but one later publicly changed his mind after being captured and thrown into jail by the British. The ink is very faded now, but luckily copies were made.

In CONGRESS, July 4, 1776.

The unanimous Declaration of the thirteen united States of America.

HIDDEN FROM THE BRITS

During the War of 1812 (see page 6), the Declaration document was smuggled out of town and taken by cart upriver to a disused mill, then by farm wagon to a private house in Leesburg, Virginia, to be hidden safely until the danger was over. During World War II, it was kept safe in Fort Knox.

STATES UNITED

The Constitution established America's government and fundamental laws. It was signed on September 17, 1787, in Philadelphia. Up to that point, the states were a loosely connected group operating like independent countries. The new nation needed a central government to bind it together.

TEN TOP RIGHTS

The Bill of Rights added ten amendments to the constitution guaranteeing citizens' rights, such as freedom of speech and religion. It was signed on December 15, 1791. There were 14 copies made at the time, and each state got their own copy. Twelve are known to have survived, and two are missing. North Carolina's copy was stolen during the Civil War and reappeared 140 years later.

THERE ARE SOME SPELLING MISTAKES IN THE CONSTITUTION. FOR INSTANCE, PENNSYLVANIA IS MISSING AN *N*.

Congress of the United States begun and held at the City of New-York, on Wednesday the Fourth of March, one thousand seven hundred and eighty nine

SCIENTIFICALLY SAFE

The special cases that hold the Charters of Freedom have super-strong titanium frames and contain inert argon gas, which helps prevent them from crumbling with age. The temperature and humidity are kept at just the right levels to prevent them from damaging the documents.

RARE TREASURES

THE PUBLIC VAULTS ARE ALSO IN THE NATIONAL ARCHIVES, AND THEY'RE A TREASURE TROVE OF RARE DOCUMENTS. MANY ITEMS ARE KEPT SAFE HERE, INCLUDING WASHINGTON'S HANDWRITTEN LETTERS AND LINCOLN'S WAR TELEGRAMS. THERE'S ALSO A RARE 1297 VERSION OF THE MAGNA CARTA, A BILL OF RIGHTS FIRST WRITTEN IN ENGLAND IN 1215, WHICH LATER INFLUENCED THE US VERSION.

STREET STROLL

Take a stroll through the city to find some street surprises, from lucky dragons and giant chairs to historic stones, stairs, and street art. Join the sidewalk crowds to see a couple of Washington's amazing mega-parades, too.

STEPS OF BEAUTY

SPANISH STEPS

Washington folk walking up 22nd Street to S Street NW suddenly find themselves on a fairy-tale staircase in a tiny park. It's called the Spanish Steps after a famous set of stairs in the heart of Rome, Italy. The hill here was too steep for old-time carriages, so the steps were built instead, in 1911. Weddings sometimes take place here, and at the top of the stairs, there's a lion ready to spout fountain water.

SPANISH STEPS

ZERO MILESTONE

STONE WITH A STORY

ZERO MILESTONE

This 1923 granite marker is not far from the White House. It was meant to be the spot from which all roads in the US are measured but it's only used as the starting point for DC's roads. However, it does mark the starting point of a great story about America's early roads...

IN 1919, PEOPLE WANTED TO PROVE THAT YOU COULD DRIVE FROM DC TO CALIFORNIA, SO ON JULY 7, AN ARMY CONVOY SET OFF FROM THIS SPOT CARRYING WREATHS FOR THE GOVERNOR OF CALIFORNIA. THE TRUCKS FACED BROKEN BRIDGES, MUD, ROCKS, SAND, DESERT HEAT, AND MOUNTAIN COLD, BUT THEY FINALLY MADE IT TO SAN FRANCISCO ON SEPTEMBER 6.

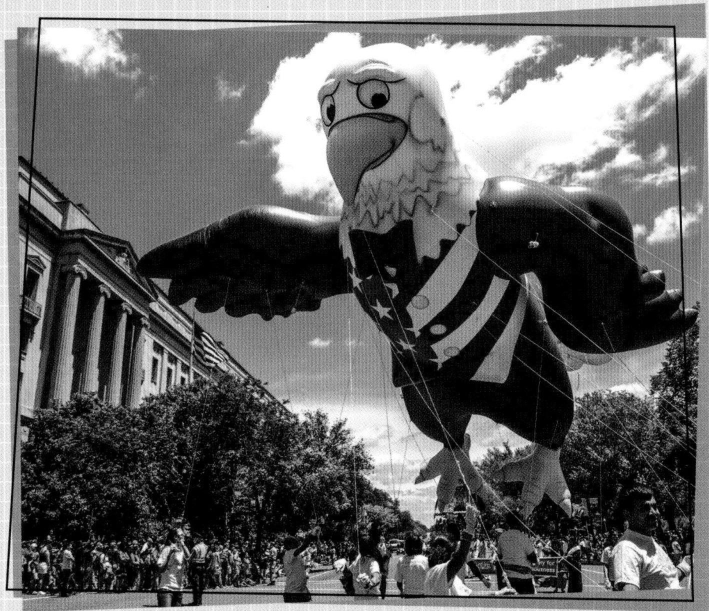

CONSTITUTION AVENUE

AMERICA'S BIRTHDAY

NATIONAL INDEPENDENCE DAY PARADE

The US's biggest annual parade wends its way along Constitution Avenue on July 4. Marching bands, army drill teams, giant balloons, floats, VIPs, and celebrities are watched by hundreds of thousands of spectators. There are representatives of all 50 states in the parade.

INDEPENDENCE DAY IS THE BIGGEST DAY OF THE YEAR FOR HOT DOGS IN THE US – AROUND 155 MILLION GET EATEN. END TO END, THAT'S ENOUGH HOT DOGS TO GO FROM WASHINGTON, DC, TO LOS ANGELES MORE THAN FIVE TIMES!

LET'S MAKE SOME NOISE

ROLLING THUNDER BIKE RALLY

In late May, on Memorial Day weekend, more than 500,000 motorcycles rev up and ride from the Pentagon to the National Mall. The ride is a tribute to prisoners of war and Americans missing in action, as well as a call to remember the needs of military veterans.

THE MALL

ALLEY OF ART

BLAGDEN ALLEY

This street is the home of the DC Alley Museum, the name given to the outdoor display of murals that artists have created here. Brightly colored portraits of local people and performers have been painted on the roll-down metal gates of the alley, which once housed horses and hansom cabs (horse-drawn carriages that were early taxis) in the 1800s. Now it's vibrant with street art.

GOLDEN GATE

FRIENDSHIP ARCH

Friendship Arch is one of the largest Chinese arches in the world. It marks the entrance to DC's small Chinatown area of Asian restaurants. It has seven roofs and parts of it are painted in 23-carat gold. The gold represents wealth and honor. The Chinese characters in the center mean "Chinese District."

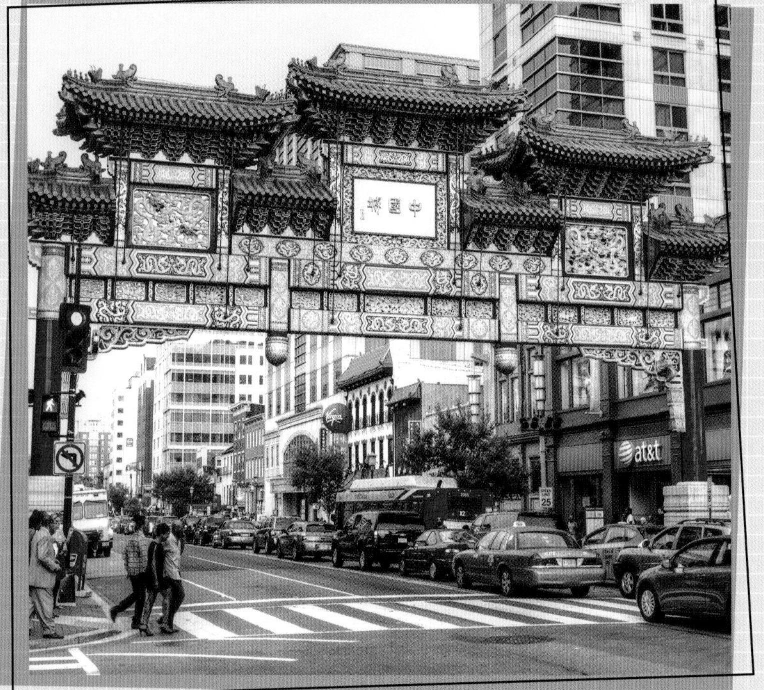

12
NUMBER OF LUCKY DRAGONS CARVED ON THE ARCH
272
NUMBER OF PAINTED LUCKY DRAGONS

ANACOSTIA

HYATTSVILLE

FURNITURE FOR GIANTS

THE BIG CHAIR

This giant chair is a famous symbol of the Anacostia neighborhood. It was first built in 1959 as an advertisement for a DC furniture company. It was the biggest chair in the world at the time. At first it was made of wood, but when it began to rot, a new chair was made of aluminum.

IN 1960, A WOMAN LIVED ON TOP OF THE CHAIR FOR 42 DAYS WITHOUT COMING DOWN, AS A PUBLICITY STUNT FOR THE FURNITURE COMPANY. SHE STAYED IN A GLASS HOUSE SO THAT EVERYBODY COULD SEE HER (EXCEPT WHEN SHE WENT TO THE BATHROOM).

JUNK MADE BEAUTIFUL

VANADU ART HOUSE AND CARS

Museum conservator Clarke Bedford decided to make his own home a great sidewalk sight. He decorated it with all kinds of junk to make a recycled wonderland, with everything from a copy of the *Mona Lisa* to pipes, wheel hubs, and bicycle chains. He's got four working cars, too. They're decorated with items such as washing machine parts, moose antlers, and graveyard spires.

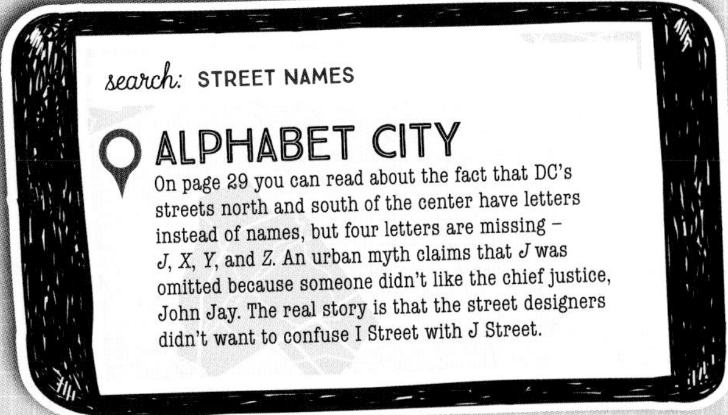

search: STREET NAMES

ALPHABET CITY

On page 29 you can read about the fact that DC's streets north and south of the center have letters instead of names, but four letters are missing – *J*, *X*, *Y*, and *Z*. An urban myth claims that *J* was omitted because someone didn't like the chief justice, John Jay. The real story is that the street designers didn't want to confuse I Street with J Street.

POWERFUL PLACES

Washington, DC, is the center of US government and politics. Take this power trail around some of the places where politicians and diplomats meet and make deals. After all, you'll need to know your way around when you become one of the world's rulers!

THE PENTAGON

HARRY S. TRUMAN BUILDING

MILITARY MILES

THE PENTAGON

The Pentagon is the home of the US Department of Defense. It's one of the world's largest office buildings, even though it was built in just 16 months, between 1941 and 1942. Its name means "five-sided," and it has five segments joined by over 17 miles (27.3 km) of hallways. Pity the poor people in the mailroom – over 1.2 million items are sent and received every month by the Pentagon!

search: PENTAGON FACTS

25,000+
the number of employees in the building.

1 MILLION
the number of e-mails sent daily from the building.

4,500
the number of cups of coffee drunk daily by the employees in the building, along with 1,700 pints of milk.

There's enough telephone wire in the Pentagon to wrap around the Earth four times.

TOP TREASURES

DIPLOMATIC RECEPTION ROOMS

Based in the Harry S. Truman Building, the State Department handles America's relations with the rest of the world. There are 42 reception rooms for signing treaties and entertaining visitors. The rooms contain 5,000 valuable objects from the 1700s and early 1800s, guaranteed to impress guests.

In the collection:

> Fine gold goblets from the 1800s

> A silver teapot made by US Revolutionary hero Paul Revere

> Some of George Washington's china

> The desk where the treaty was signed that ended the American Revolution in 1783

SCOTTISH RITE TEMPLE

TEMPLE OF MYSTERIES

SCOTTISH RITE TEMPLE

This building is home to the Freemasons, one of the world's biggest supposedly secret societies. It has two sphinxes, representing Wisdom and Power, guarding the entrance. There are lots of strange symbols around the building, including gilded serpents, a throne, and a stained-glass window that shows a mysterious "all-seeing eye." No wonder novelists and filmmakers love creating stories about it! Now anyone can take a guided tour.

EMBASSY ROW

GOING ABROAD AT HOME

EMBASSY ROW

It's possible to go to more than 170 countries without leaving Washington, DC, because it's home to over 170 embassies from around the world. Visitors who step inside an embassy technically enter a foreign country, as the grounds are an extension of that embassy's nation. Many of them are in the fine homes that once belonged to DC's millionaires on a stretch of Massachusetts Avenue called Embassy Row.

THE WHITE HOUSE

PRESIDENT'S PAD

THE WHITE HOUSE

The president's house was first built between 1792 and 1800. Legend has it that after the British burned the building in the War of 1812, the house was restored and painted white to cover the smoke marks. That's not true – it's always been white.

OUT OF IRELAND

Architect James Hoban wanted to make the building simple, so as not to seem too royal. He modeled it on Leinster House, a mid-18th-century duke's villa in Dublin, Ireland, that still stands and is now used by Ireland's Parliament.

PRESIDENTIAL ADD-ONS

Presidents have customized the property over time. Franklin Roosevelt added a swimming pool. Richard Nixon added a bowling alley. Bill Clinton added a jogging track, and Barack Obama added a vegetable garden. There's also a movie theater, a game room, and a tennis court.

412 DOORS

132 ROOMS

147 WINDOWS

FIRST OFFICE

The president works in the Oval Office, and each new president gets to add decorations of their own, such as paintings and sculptures. They can also have the rug redesigned. It always has the Presidential Seal at its center, but the border can show different themes.

HOUSE IN THE HOUSE

Thirty-ninth president Jimmy Carter's daughter Amy had her own tree house in the White House grounds. Secret Service agents made sure that she and her friends were safe when they had sleepovers!

THE PRESIDENTIAL SEAL SHOWS A BALD EAGLE CARRYING OLIVE BRANCHES, REPRESENTING PEACE, IN ONE TALON. IT CARRIES ARROWS, REPRESENTING MILITARY MIGHT, IN THE OTHER.

EASTER EGG ROLL

THERE'S BEEN AN EASTER EGG ROLL AT THE WHITE HOUSE SINCE THE 1800S. NOW, 35,000 TICKETS ARE DISTRIBUTED BY A LOTTERY FOR THE EVENT, HELD ON EASTER MONDAY. CHILDREN AND THEIR PARENTS CAN TRY THEIR HAND AT ROLLING AN EGG ON THE GRASS WITH A LONG-HANDLED SPOON, AND THERE'S AN EGG HUNT, TOO. A WHOPPING 14,500 EGGS ARE USED OVERALL, AND THE CHILDREN WHO TAKE PART GET TO TAKE HOME A WOODEN EGG SOUVENIR.

CONGRESS PASSED A LAW IN 1876 TO BAN THE EGG ROLL AROUND THE CAPITOL BUILDING. THEY DIDN'T WANT IT MESSING UP THE GRASS.

HISTORY'S HOTEL

WILLARD HOTEL

Washington is the home of politics, and this hotel has been a meeting place for politicians since the days of Abraham Lincoln. Lots of presidents have slept here, their heads no doubt full of political deal-making! Martin Luther King Jr. finished his "I Have a Dream" speech in the hotel, and author Mark Twain wrote two books here.

FBI ADDRESS

J. EDGAR HOOVER BUILDING

This imposing building is home to the Federal Bureau of Investigation, the FBI. This is the US government department that investigates terrorism, spying, cyber warfare, corruption, and organized crime. It puts together America's Ten Most Wanted list of criminals.

J. EDGAR HOOVER BUILDING

HOME OF THE DOME

THE CAPITOL

The Capitol is the building where Congress meets, making it the center of US government. The central room – under the dome – is the Rotunda. A painted frieze around the rim of the inside shows more than 400 years of American history, with figures 15 ft. (4.5 m) tall so they can be seen from below. The dome is made from cast iron bolted together and painted white.

IN 2002, SECURITY CAMERAS CAPTURED THE IMAGE OF A WILD FOX THAT WANDERED INTO THE BUILDING. IT STAYED HIDDEN FOR 24 HOURS BEFORE IT WAS CAUGHT.

540
THE NUMBER OF ROOMS

Members of Congress used to take baths in marble tubs in the basement back in the 1800s.

COURT WITH A COURT

SUPREME COURT

The Supreme Court is known as "The Highest Court in the Land," but strictly speaking, there's an even higher one. Three floors above the courtroom there's a basketball court for use by employees. The only restriction is that they're not allowed to play on court days – the sound of a ball being bounced might be a bit off-putting! There's a gym, too, for times when the nation's top justices and other workers want to work out.

ONLY IN DC

This is a trail like no other. It will take you via some of Washington's most unique locations and objects. Prepare for some surprises, a few gasps, and one or two shivers as you discover some DC specials.

GROSS ALERT!

NATIONAL MUSEUM OF HEALTH AND MEDICINE

This museum was founded during the Civil War to collect specimens that would help medical research. It does great work, but some of its exhibits are not for the fainthearted!

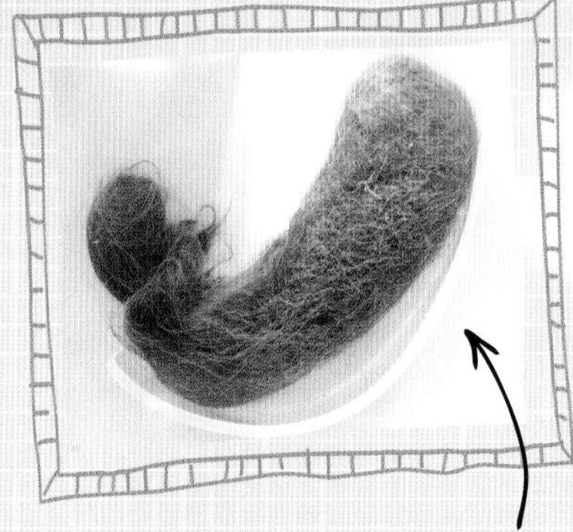

A STOMACH-SHAPED HUMAN HAIRBALL TAKEN FROM A 12-YEAR-OLD GIRL WITH A HABIT OF EATING HER HAIR.

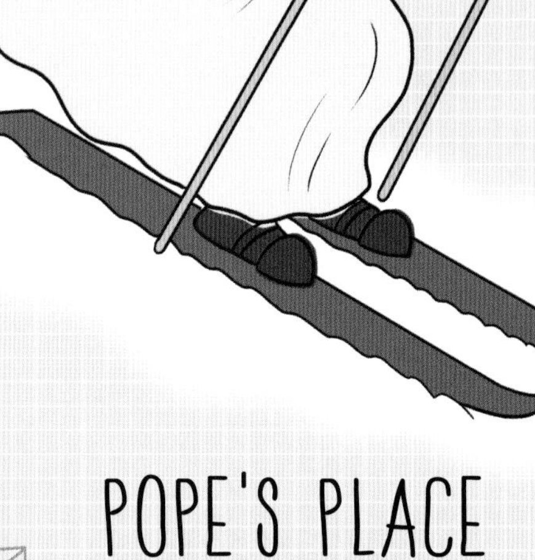

THE MANGLED LEG OF MAJOR GENERAL DANIEL E. SICKLES, SHATTERED BY A CANNONBALL AT THE BATTLE OF GETTYSBURG.

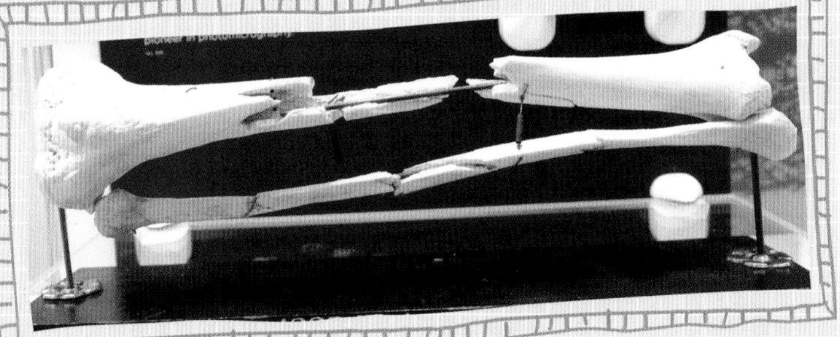

POPE'S PLACE

SAINT JOHN PAUL II NATIONAL SHRINE

This papal shrine is in memory of Saint John Paul II, who was pope from 1978 to 2005. A sample of his blood is contained inside a glass ampule in an ornate container, and a pair of his skis are on display, too.

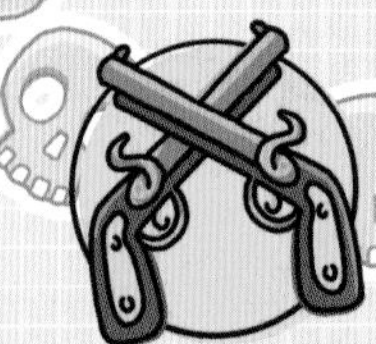

NATIONAL MUSEUM OF HEALTH AND MEDICINE

SAINT JOHN PAUL II NATIONAL SHRINE

ROME'S TOMBS

FRANCISCAN MONASTERY

At the end of the 1800s, the friars of the Franciscan Monastery brought Rome to DC. They built a reproduction of the Catacombs of Rome, tomb tunnels under the Italian city of Rome where early Christians were buried. Visitors can explore dark, narrow passages that wind past some fake tombs and the real remains of St. Innocent and St. Benignus. They were both killed in Ancient Rome for being Christian.

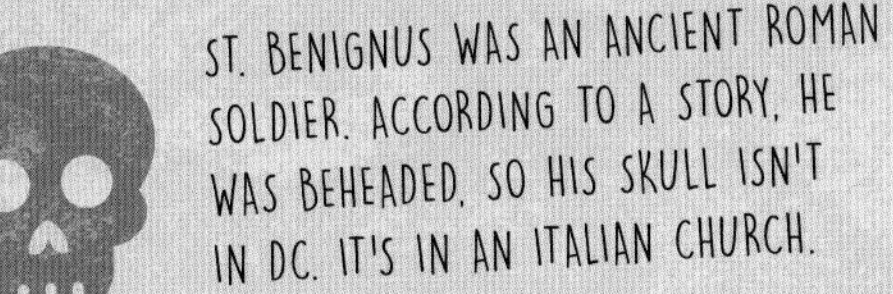

ST. BENIGNUS WAS AN ANCIENT ROMAN SOLDIER. ACCORDING TO A STORY, HE WAS BEHEADED, SO HIS SKULL ISN'T IN DC. IT'S IN AN ITALIAN CHURCH.

EVERYBODY, RIDE!

THE SMITHSONIAN CAROUSEL

Sixty horses, one of them a beautiful sea dragon hybrid, live on the Mall. For decades they have been taking children for a ride on the Smithsonian Carousel. The carousel was once in a Baltimore amusement park, where African American children were not allowed. On the same day as Martin Luther King Jr.'s "I Have a Dream" speech (see page 9), segregation was ended in the park, and the carousel was opened to all. It's a symbol of unity, as well as a beloved landmark.

search: WORLD NEWS

HOLD THE FRONT PAGE

You can take a look at the world's headlines every day without even leaving DC – the Newseum picks 80 front pages from over 800 they receive each day from newsrooms in other countries, and displays them in a special gallery.

DC'S STASH OF SECRETS

INTERNATIONAL SPY MUSEUM

One of the largest collections of spy equipment in the world is on display here. There are hidden cameras in pens and buttons, hidden guns in gloves and lipsticks, and all sorts of other ingenious ways of gathering and hiding secrets. One of the most unusual highlights is a pigeon camera – a tiny camera fitted to pigeons during World War I to snap pictures from the air.

OLD NEWS

NEWSEUM

This museum is dedicated to freedom of speech and to the work of journalists. It has unique artifacts associated with important news stories, such as the fall of the Berlin Wall in 1989. On display there are eight 12 ft. (3.6 m) high sections of the wall, which once divided East and West Berlin. There's also a three-story guard tower once manned by East German guards, who would shoot anyone who tried to escape across the wall from East to West.

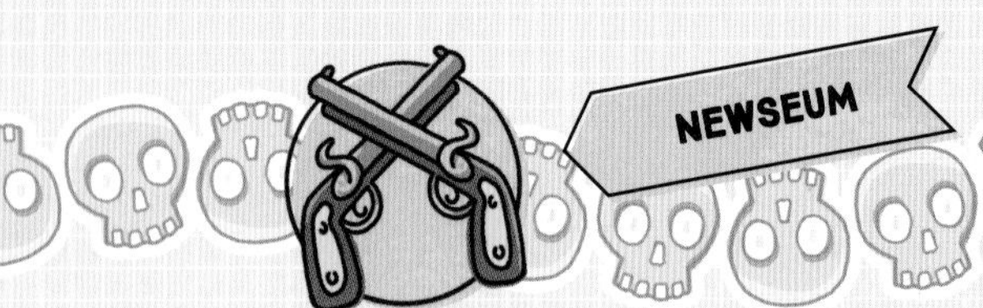

THE GUN THAT KILLED LINCOLN

FORD'S THEATRE

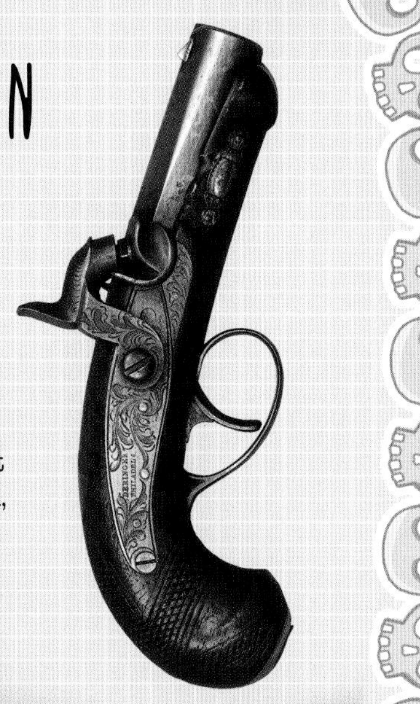

On April 14, 1865, John Wilkes Booth assassinated Abraham Lincoln in his box seat at this theater. There's now a museum in the basement of the theater where Booth's pistol and his muddy boot are on display, along with Lincoln's clothes. The Civil War had just come to an end when Lincoln was killed, and Booth thought he was benefiting the South by his action. In fact, the assassination made the aftermath of the war worse for the South, not better.

WHEN THE ARGUING GOT SERIOUS

BLADENSBURG DUELING GROUNDS

During the 1800s, countless duels were fought here. Washington politicians, military men, and local gentlemen fought and sometimes killed each other over all kinds of arguments. The dueling grounds were over the border in Maryland because dueling was illegal in DC itself. A plaque now marks the spot beside a creek that once had the grisly nickname "Blood Run."

BLADENSBURG DUELING GROUNDS

EAT THE STREETS

Washington has many food cultures and traditions. This trail picks out a few tasty examples to make you feel hungry for a plate of capital treats.

AFRICAN AMERICANS WERE NOT SERVED IN MANY DC RESTAURANTS UNTIL 1953. THIS UNFAIR TREATMENT BASED ON RACE (AKA SEGREGATION) ENDED THANKS TO MARY CHURCH TERRELL. WHEN SHE WAS REFUSED SERVICE, SHE TOOK A SEGREGATION CASE TO THE SUPREME COURT AND WON, AGED NEARLY 90.

BEN'S CHILI BOWL

THE DC SAUSAGE

HALF-SMOKE

DC's most famous food is the half-smoke, a bigger and spicier version of a hot dog. People argue over how it got its name. It could be because the sausage is usually cut down the middle, or because some sausages are half beef and half pork. It doesn't really matter as long as it's delicious! It's normally topped with chili and chopped onions. Ben's Chili Bowl makes a famous half-smoke.

COOKED WITH SOUL

SOUL FOOD

This African American cuisine has its origins in West Africa, but was adapted by slaves when they reached the US. Popular dishes include fried chicken, spareribs, mac and cheese, collard greens, catfish, pigs' feet, and sweet potato pie. Washington's Florida Avenue Grill claims to be the oldest soul food restaurant in the world.

FLORIDA AVENUE GRILL

OUT OF AFRICA

LITTLE ETHIOPIA

The DC region is home to the largest number of Ethiopians outside Africa, and they have brought their food culture with them. A stretch of 9th Street NW in the Shaw neighborhood is known as Little Ethiopia because of the many Ethiopian restaurants and businesses there. Ethiopian food is eaten with *injera*, a spongy flatbread, which is used in place of cutlery and sometimes even used as a plate.

SOME OF THE ETHIOPIAN DISHES FOUND IN DC

~ *ENKULAL TIBS* ~
A TASTY BREAKFAST OF SCRAMBLED EGGS, PEPPERS, TOMATOES, AND ONION

~ *FUL* ~
CHICKPEAS MASHED WITH BUTTER

~ *WA* ~
A SPICY CURRY

~ *AIB* ~
COTTAGE CHEESE

EAT THE PLANET

UNION MARKET

This indoor market has something yummy for everyone. With 40 different food sellers, you can taste your way around the world here. Start your journey in the East with Taiwanese ramen (noodle soup), Burmese *falooda* (milkshakes), or Indian *dosas* (pancakes). There are South American empanadas (stuffed pastries), Mexican tacos, Asian tea, barbecue fare, and plenty of other tasty treats from around the globe for gourmets to gobble up!

THE RULING SOUP

SENATE BEAN SOUP

This special soup has been on the menu in the Senate's restaurant for over 100 years. It's a broth of beans, ham hock, and onions. Nobody knows for sure which senator first asked for the soup, but it's been served since 1903.

Presidents' favorite dishes

Abraham Lincoln
Gingerbread

Thomas Jefferson
Waffles

Franklin D. Roosevelt
Hot dogs

Richard Nixon
Meatloaf

Bill Clinton
Cheeseburgers

George W. Bush
Huevos rancheros

NOT ON THE MENU

WHITE HOUSE TURKEY PARDON

On Thanksgiving Day in November, there's normally a meal of roast turkey, but there's also a tradition of saving a turkey or two. The president officially pardons one or two turkeys each year, and they are given names by White House staff. In 2016, Tater and Tot were saved. In 2015, it was Abe and Honest, and in 2014, it was Cheese and Mac. The saved birds live out their days on a farm, safe from the plate.

MARTHA WASHINGTON, WIFE OF GEORGE, WAS WELL KNOWN LOCALLY FOR HER GREAT CAKE, A KIND OF RICH FRUITCAKE. IT'S SOMETIMES CALLED WASHINGTON CAKE.

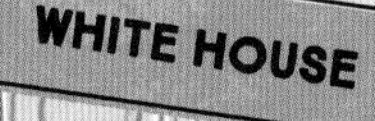

CRAB CENTRAL

MAINE AVENUE FISH MARKET

Welcome to the oldest operating open-air fish market in the US. Here, the vendors sell fish, crabs, oysters, and other seafood so fresh it's almost still swimming. Locals sit eating their favorite cooked fish on the waterfront benches, keeping an eye out for thieving seagulls. It's the place to try the local specialty of blue crabs.

NATIONAL MUSEUM OF THE AMERICAN INDIAN

MAINE AVENUE FISH MARKET

NATIVE AMERICAN MENU

NATIONAL MUSEUM OF THE AMERICAN INDIAN

The museum's Mitsitam Café serves Native American dishes from different regions, using ingredients produced by Native American people. There's wild salmon from the northwest coast and buffalo chili on frybread from the Great Plains. Maple-brined turkey and wild rice come from the northern woodlands, while chicken tamales come from South America.

search: MITSITAM CAFÉ
TOTEM
The café has its own 20 ft. (6 m) high totem pole carved by a Tlingit artist from Alaska.
MITSITAM
The restaurant's name means "Let's eat" in the Piscataway and Delaware languages.
MENU
The Native American food served is a mix of authentic traditional and modern dishes.

THE GREEN SCENE

Washington isn't all about important buildings and monuments. There are some awesome plants, too. Put on your gardening boots to discover the leafy secrets of DC.

FLOWER POWER

NATIONAL CHERRY BLOSSOM FESTIVAL

Washington, DC, is famous for its beautiful cherry trees, which line the Potomac riverbanks and bloom around the Washington Monument and National Mall. Everyone waits eagerly to hear news of the trees beginning to flower because it's a sure sign of springtime. The whole city celebrates with the National Cherry Blossom Festival. It runs for three weeks between the end of March and the beginning of April.

1.5 MILLION
NUMBER OF PEOPLE WHO VISIT THE TREES DURING FESTIVAL TIME

PEOPLE CAN GET MARRIED UNDER THE BLOSSOMING TREES

THANK YOU, JAPAN

Japan is world famous for its beautiful and epic displays of cherry blossoms. In 1912, the mayor of Tokyo gave 3,000 cherry trees to Washington, DC, as a gift of friendship between Japan and the US. The National Cherry Blossom Festival celebrates that friendship.

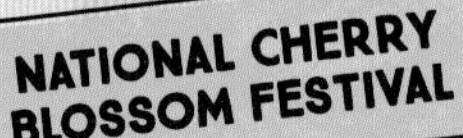

BIG BLOSSOM DAY

"Peak bloom" is when the largest number of trees flower at the same time. The average peak bloom in recent years has been around March 31. Warm weather makes it happen earlier (March 15, 1990, is the record). Cold weather makes it happen later (April 18, 1958, wins the prize for lateness).

THE FLOWER PARADE

The festival ends with a big parade led by two young women chosen as the US and Japanese Cherry Blossom Queens. The US queen is selected from Cherry Blossom Princesses representing different states and territories. She's chosen randomly, by the spinning of a wheel.

KNOW YOUR TREES

There are two types of flowering cherry trees on display. The Yoshino has white blossoms and the Kwanzan has pink flowers. There's a blossom cam that shows pictures online, so you can see the trees in bloom even if you don't visit.

TIME TO LIGHT

A 360-year-old Japanese stone lantern is lit once a year for the festival. It stands on the Tidal Basin. Centuries ago, it would have been lit to honor a shogun, one of Japan's military rulers in the 1600s.

KITE FIGHTING FUN

THE BLOSSOM KITE FESTIVAL IS PART OF THE CELEBRATIONS. THE ROKKAKU BATTLE FEATURES HEXAGONAL-SHAPED JAPANESE FIGHTER KITES. TEAMS OF KITE FLIERS TRY TO CUT THE STRING OR FORCE OPPOSING KITES TO THE GROUND. IN THE HOT TRICKS SHOWDOWN EVENT, KITE FLIERS COMPETE ONE-ON-ONE, FLYING THEIR KITES TO MUSIC. THE WINNER IS THE COMPETITOR WHO GETS THE LOUDEST APPLAUSE FROM THE AUDIENCE.

TEDDY'S ISLAND

THEODORE ROOSEVELT ISLAND

This wooded island in the Potomac is a wilderness reserve dedicated to the 26th president, Theodore Roosevelt, who was eager to protect the environment. There are no cars or bikes allowed in this peaceful spot – very different to how it was in 1898, when it was a test range for explosives like dynamite!

THEODORE ROOSEVELT ISLAND

STRANGE AND SHINY GLASS FOREST

PALISADES PARK

An unusual and magical location is hidden along a trail in the woods at Palisades Park. It's an art forest, made from sculptures that use recycled materials. Pieces of mirror, glass, metal, sticks, pipes, and all kinds of other surprising bits and pieces hang from the branches, swaying and chiming in the wind.

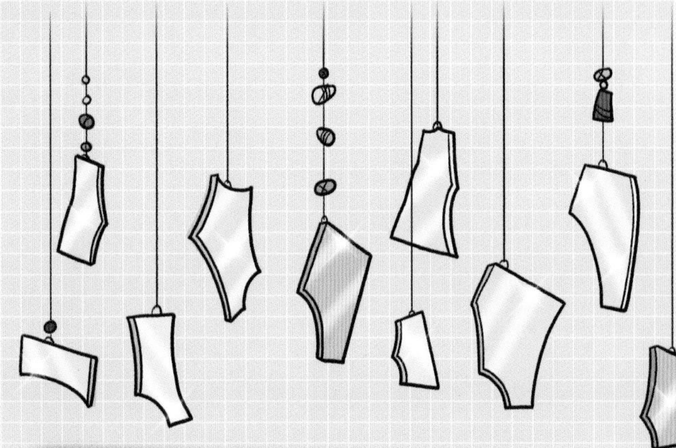

search: TREE FACTS

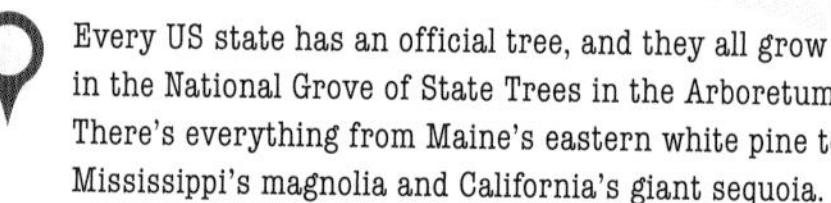

- Every US state has an official tree, and they all grow in the National Grove of State Trees in the Arboretum. There's everything from Maine's eastern white pine to Mississippi's magnolia and California's giant sequoia.
- The sugar maple is the tree of four states – New York, West Virginia, Wisconsin, and Vermont.
- The official national tree of the US is the oak.

HISTORY'S HERBS

BISHOP'S GARDEN

A medieval garden has been re-created next to the National Cathedral. Lining its lovely pathways there are plants that were grown for medicinal use by monks a thousand years ago. To help decide what to plant, the garden designers read a poem by a German monk called Walafrid Strabo. Around 1,200 years ago, he wrote about the plants he grew in his abbey garden, and the medicines he made from them, such as mint to help cure a sore throat and radishes to cure a cough.

BISHOP'S GARDEN

MINI-MASTERPIECES

NATIONAL ARBORETUM

The National Bonsai and Penjing Museum is part of the National Arboretum. Bonsai is the art of growing mini-trees, and Penjing is the art of pruning them into mini-landscapes. There's also a collection of viewing stones. These are stones that are thought interesting to look at because they resemble natural features, such as waterfalls and mountains.

IN 2014, TWO BALD EAGLES ARRIVED TO NEST IN ONE OF THE TREES IN THE ARBORETUM. THEY'VE BEEN GIVEN THE NAMES MR. PRESIDENT AND THE FIRST LADY AND HAVE BEEN RAISING CHICKS EVERY YEAR SINCE THEN. THERE'S AN EAGLE CAM SO PEOPLE CAN SEE THEIR NEST EACH YEAR.

WATERY WONDERLAND

KENILWORTH AQUATIC GARDENS

This beautiful spot is the US's only national park devoted to water plants. There are 44 ponds filled with water lilies and lotus plants. They provide the perfect DC neighborhood for birds, turtles, and frogs.

KENILWORTH AQUATIC GARDENS

THE LOTUS WAS A SACRED PLANT IN ANCIENT EGYPTIAN TIMES, AND IT'S A SYMBOL OF PURITY IN THE BUDDHIST RELIGION. IT'S CELEBRATED DURING THE PARK'S LOTUS AND WATER LILY FESTIVAL, WHEN VISITORS CAN HAVE FLOWERS PAINTED ON THEIR FACES AND DRINK LOTUS TEA.

CONGRESSIONAL CEMETERY

PRIVATE POOCH PARK

CONGRESSIONAL CEMETERY

Locals help to keep the garden tidy at this old burial ground. In return for this work, they get to walk dogs here because it doubles as a members-only dog park, where hounds can run free around the tombs and gravestones. There's a year-long waiting list to join the exclusive private pooch club. However, everybody is allowed in for the yearly Dog of the Day event, when pets get the chance to win prizes from local vets.

AT CHRISTMAS, DOGS CAN VISIT THE CEMETERY TO HAVE THEIR PHOTO TAKEN WITH SANTA.

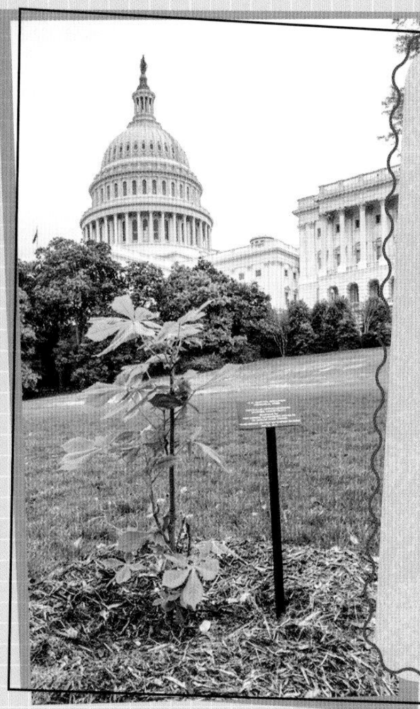

WASHINGTON'S HOLOCAUST MEMORIAL MUSEUM HAS A SPECIAL EXHIBITION FOR CHILDREN OVER EIGHT TO SEE, CALLED *REMEMBER THE CHILDREN: DANIEL'S STORY*. IT EXPLAINS HOW JEWISH CHILDREN WERE TREATED BY THE NAZIS DURING WORLD WAR II. THERE ARE ALSO 3,000 TILE PANELS ON DISPLAY, MADE BY AMERICAN SCHOOLCHILDREN TO HONOR THE VICTIMS.

OTHER WORLDS IN WASHINGTON

UNITED STATES BOTANIC GARDEN

There's a place where you can visit a tropical rainforest, a scorching desert, or even the land of the dinosaurs, right in the heart of DC. These are some of the plant landscapes re-created at the US Botanic Garden. In the Garden Primeval, you can walk among ferns and other ancient plants from 150 million years ago, and imagine a giant dinosaur such as a stegosaurus or a brachiosaurus just around the corner!

UNITED STATES BOTANIC GARDEN

THERE ARE SOME EVER-HUNGRY MONSTERS LIVING AT THE US BOTANIC GARDEN. IT HAS A COLLECTION OF MEAT-EATING PLANTS THAT TRAP INSECTS AND EAT THEM!

A REMEMBERING TREE

ANNE FRANK TREE

Anne Frank was a Jewish girl from the Netherlands. She and her family went into hiding from the Nazis during World War II. During two years of hiding in a secret attic, she wrote a diary that later became famous. Eventually, they were betrayed, and Anne died in a concentration camp. Only her father survived, and saved her diaries. While she hid, all she could see of the outside world was part of a chestnut tree. Chestnuts from the tree were later collected and germinated, and one of them was planted outside the Capitol building as a powerful memory of Anne Frank's story.

ANNE FRANK TREE

WIN WASHINGTON

Take a tour of Washington's sports teams and surprising competitive contests. Could you cook up a winning barbecue sauce or spell the word "Gesellschaft"? If so, you could be a DC winner, too.

START

GO, PRES!

THE RACING PRESIDENTS

The Washington Nationals have hosted the famous Racing Presidents event since 2006. In the middle of the fourth inning, people in giant-headed, foam-rubber costumes of George Washington, Abraham Lincoln, Thomas Jefferson, Teddy Roosevelt, and William Taft waddle out onto the field for a race, along with a guest president chosen each year.

TEDDY ROOSEVELT LOST 525 RACES IN A ROW, UNTIL HE FINALLY WON IN 2012. HE DELIGHTED THE CROWD BY TRYING EVER MORE OUTLANDISH WAYS TO WIN, SUCH AS A ZIPWIRE, A GOLF CART, AND A RICKSHAW!

COOK UP A WIN

GIANT BARBECUE BATTLE

At this big summer cooking and music festival, crowds come to Pennsylvania Avenue to see teams from around the country cook off against each other in the Giant National Barbecue Championship. There are big cash prizes to be won in cooking categories using beef, chicken, pork, and lamb. There's a chance for budding barbecue chefs to win the Nation's Best Barbecue Sauce contest, too.

THE BLACK-AND-RED

DC UNITED

When Major League Soccer was created in the mid-1990s, Washington was given the first franchise. The team is nicknamed the Black-and-Red, the colors of their uniform. The team mascot is an eagle called Talon. The games are famous for the pre-match fun had by everyone in the parking lot outside, where the crowd likes to tuck into Central and South American food such as *pupusas* (stuffed tortillas), sold from food trucks.

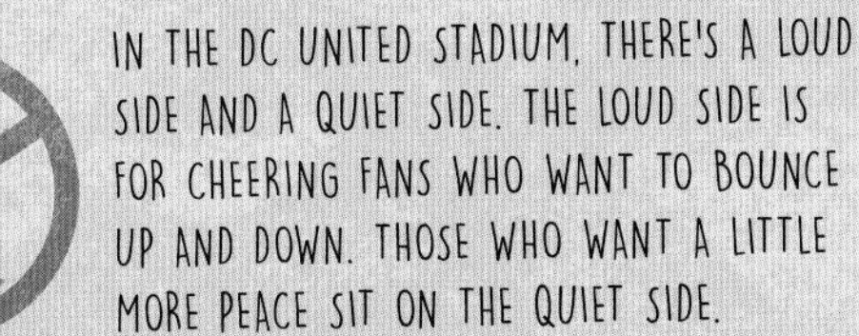

IN THE DC UNITED STADIUM, THERE'S A LOUD SIDE AND A QUIET SIDE. THE LOUD SIDE IS FOR CHEERING FANS WHO WANT TO BOUNCE UP AND DOWN. THOSE WHO WANT A LITTLE MORE PEACE SIT ON THE QUIET SIDE.

RFK STADIUM

WILLIAMS WINS

WASHINGTON REDSKINS

Washington's NFL team is the capital's best-known sports team internationally. They've won the Super Bowl three times. When they won in 1988, they famously fielded Doug Williams, the first African American quarterback ever to appear in the Super Bowl. He played a storming game to beat the Denver Broncos, even though he'd endured a four-hour dental operation the day before!

MANY PEOPLE WANT WASHINGTON'S FOOTBALL TEAM TO CHANGE ITS NAME AND LOGO BECAUSE IT'S CONSIDERED OFFENSIVE TO THE NATIVE AMERICAN COMMUNITY.

WASHINGTON REDSKINS

BATTLE OF THE BISONS

UNIVERSITY TEAMS

Two DC universities have the same nickname for their sports teams, and they often face each other on the basketball court, football field, and athletics track. Teams for Howard University and Gallaudet University (for deaf students) are both nicknamed the "Bisons."

WHEN THE NATIONAL ZOO GOT TWO NEW BISON, IT ASKED STUDENTS FROM EACH UNIVERSITY TO COME UP WITH NAMES. HOWARD CHOSE ZORA. GALLAUDET CHOSE WILMA. BOTH ARE NAMES OF FAMOUS FORMER STUDENTS.

VERIZON CENTER

RECORD BREAKERS

CAPITALS ICE HOCKEY

The Capitals ice hockey team plays in the Verizon Center. Its mascot is a skating bald eagle called Slapshot, who wears a jersey with the number 00 on it. When the Capitals first started, in the 1974–1975 season, they were so awful they became known as one of the worst US pro sports teams of all time. They set all sorts of worst-ever records, losing 17 matches in a row and 39 out of 40 away games. Most of those records still stand, but the team is much more successful now.

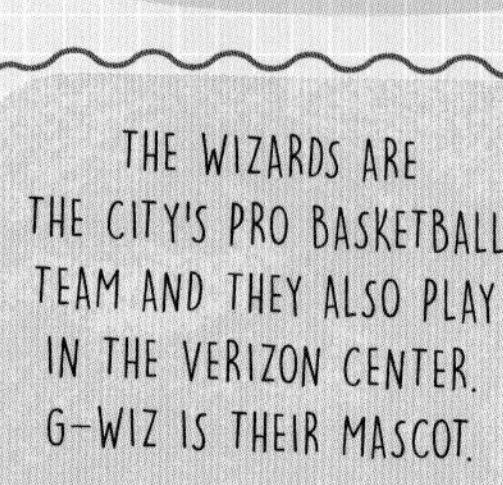

THE WIZARDS ARE THE CITY'S PRO BASKETBALL TEAM AND THEY ALSO PLAY IN THE VERIZON CENTER. G-WIZ IS THEIR MASCOT.

ALL OVER WASHINGTON

RUN FOR EVERYONE

MARINE CORPS MARATHON

The US Marine Corps runs this marathon, starting and finishing near Arlington. It's nicknamed the "People's Marathon" because it's the largest marathon in the world that doesn't offer prize money. It's for ordinary people who want to improve their fitness, rather than for professional runners. Around 30,000 people take part on the day, but members of the armed forces can run it from afar. They can get their marathon medals by running the race remotely on army bases, ship decks, embassy compounds, and air bases around the world.

SPLENDIFEROUS SPELLING

NATIONAL SPELLING BEE

Every year, 11 million children take part in the National Spelling Bee, a spelling contest that began in 1925. The finals are held just outside DC in National Harbor in Maryland, and the winner gets $40,000 plus other prizes, such as savings bonds and books. Over the years, the winners have been equally split between boys and girls.

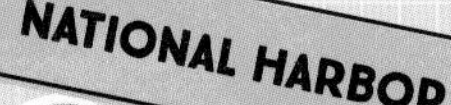

National Spelling Bee

- The final is televised on a national sports channel.
- No one knows exactly why the contest is called a bee.
- Words for the contest are taken from *Webster's Third New International Dictionary*. There are 472,000 to choose from.

Some winning words in recent years:

cymotrichous

feuilleton

stichomythia

scherenschnitte

Feldenkrais

gesellschaft

LOOK UP!

Washington, DC, may not have the tallest skyscrapers in the country, but there are plenty of great things to look up at! Turn your eyes skyward to discover some great stories.

60,000

APPROX. NUMBER OF OBJECTS IN THE COLLECTION

Ranging in size from giant Saturn V space rockets to tiny microchips.

FLYING HIGH

NATIONAL AIR AND SPACE MUSEUM

The Smithsonian's largest museum holds the world's biggest collection of aviation and space artifacts. It's spread over two sites, one in the heart of the city and one at the Udvar-Hazy Center a couple of miles away in Virginia. It's the place to see some of the most famous record-breaking aircraft and spaceships that have ever flown, many hanging from the ceilings. The museum has a record of its own, too. It's the US's most-visited museum.

NATIONAL AIR AND SPACE MUSEUM

THE FIRST FLIGHT WAS PILOTED BY ORVILLE WRIGHT. THE PLANE TOOK 12 SECONDS TO TRAVEL 120 FT. (36 M).

THE FIRST FLIGHT

The *Wright Flyer*, the first powered aircraft ever to fly, is on display at the museum. It first took off in 1903 at Kitty Hawk, North Carolina. The Wright brothers, Orville and Wilbur, built and flew it.

ACROSS THE POND

One of the most popular exhibits is the *Spirit of St. Louis*, the single-engine monoplane flown by Charles Lindbergh on the first-ever nonstop flight across the Atlantic, in 1927. Lindbergh flew from New York to Paris, where a crowd of 100,000 excited people were waiting to congratulate him. He loved his tough little plane and said it was like a living creature.

BACK FROM THE MOON

VISITORS CAN SEE A SPACECRAFT THAT REACHED THE HEIGHTS OF SPACEFLIGHT ACHIEVEMENT AND RETURNED SAFELY, CARRYING ITS PRECIOUS CARGO OF THREE FAMOUS ASTRONAUTS. THE APOLLO 11 COMMAND MODULE, *COLUMBIA*, BROUGHT NEIL ARMSTRONG, EDWIN "BUZZ" ALDRIN, AND MICHAEL COLLINS BACK FROM THE FIRST LANDING ON THE MOON. IT SPLASHED DOWN IN THE PACIFIC OCEAN ON JULY 24, 1969.

LITTLE RED BUS

In 1932, Amelia Earhart flew her red Lockheed 5B Vega across the Atlantic, and later the US, solo. She was the first woman to achieve either feat, and the second person to fly across the Atlantic solo. She called the plane her “little red bus.” It’s now on display in the museum.

WASHINGTON MONUMENT

LIBRARY OF CONGRESS

LEARN FROM THE CEILINGS

LIBRARY OF CONGRESS

Anyone visiting the Thomas Jefferson Building, part of the Library of Congress, will be inspired to learn and achieve just by looking upward. The ceiling of the Great Hall is painted with lots of quotations from famous writers. The Main Reading Room has a giant dome decorated with murals celebrating human strengths and achievements.

ON THE DOMED CEILING, THERE ARE WINGED FIGURES, REPRESENTING THE ACHIEVEMENTS OF VARIOUS COUNTRIES. THE US IS REPRESENTED BY AN ENGINEER SITTING BEHIND AN ELECTRIC DYNAMO (MACHINE), SHOWING THE COUNTRY'S CONTRIBUTION TO TECHNOLOGY.

TIP TOP

TOP OF THE WASHINGTON MONUMENT

At the very top of the Washington Monument there is a 9 in. (23 cm) cast aluminum pyramid, installed to act as a lightning conductor. At the time the monument was built, in the late 1800s, aluminum was rare and expensive. Before the shiny novelty went to its Washington home, it was displayed as a treasure in the window of famous New York jewelry store Tiffany's. The words *Laus Deo* (Praise be to God) are engraved on the tip. It was added to the monument during a ceremony, while gale force winds howled around the scaffolding!

IT CAME FROM OUTER SPACE

NATIONAL CATHEDRAL SPACE WINDOW

A small piece of 3.6-billion-year-old rock from the moon is embedded in one of the cathedral's stained-glass windows. It is encased in an airtight, nitrogen-filled capsule in the center of the window. It was brought back by the astronauts of Apollo 11, the first space mission to land on the moon (see page 63).

THE STAINED-GLASS ARTIST RODNEY WINFIELD TOOK HIS INSPIRATION FOR THE CATHEDRAL WINDOW BY LOOKING AT PHOTOS TAKEN BY THE APOLLO II CREW IN SPACE.

PERFECT PLANE POINT

GRAVELLY POINT PARK

This spot in Arlington, near Reagan National Airport, is where airplane fans come for roaring, shaking, close-up views of planes taking off and landing. The engines deafen as jetliners zoom overhead, taking off from or landing on the nearby runway. When the wind blows from the north, plane spotters see aircraft taking off, but when the wind comes from the south, the planes come in to land over the park.

PRESIDENT'S PILE

TOWER OF BOOKS, FORD'S THEATRE

There's a pile of books 34 ft. (10.36 m) high in the Ford's Theatre Center for Education and Leadership. The books are made of aluminum, and the tower includes 205 titles about Abraham Lincoln that are repeated throughout. There are approximately 6,800 pieces (books) in the tower. Visitors can get a close look by climbing up a spiral staircase around the tower.

SEE THE STARS

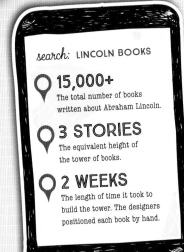

ROCK CREEK PARK PLANETARIUM

It's hard to see the stars in a big city such as Washington because light pollution blocks out the night sky view. The rangers at Rock Creek have the answer. They project Washington's night sky onto the park's planetarium dome, exactly as it would look without the light interference. The rangers have nicknamed their projector the "Seymour" – because it helps you *see more*!

search: LINCOLN BOOKS

15,000+
The total number of books written about Abraham Lincoln.

3 STORIES
The equivalent height of the tower of books.

2 WEEKS
The length of time it took to build the tower. The designers positioned each book by hand.

SAY IT WITH FLAGS

NAVY MEMORIAL SIGNAL FLAGS

Beside the Navy Memorial, on Pennsylvania Avenue NW, there are two flagpoles that look like ships' masts. Ships' signal flags are displayed on the poles. They were once used to send messages between boats, and each flag represents a letter. Together they spell out U-S-N-A-V-Y-M-E-M-O-R-I-A-L.

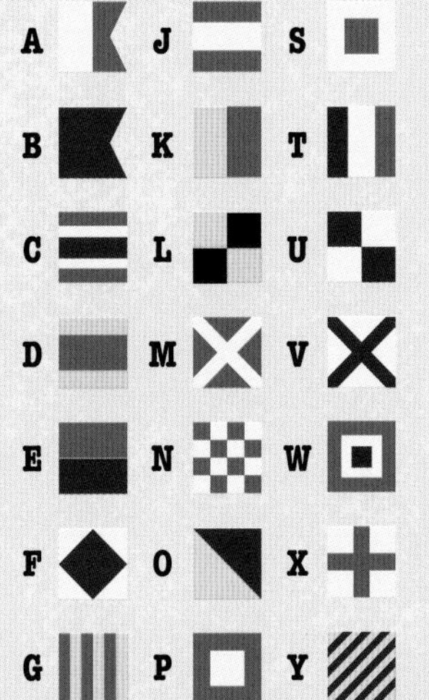

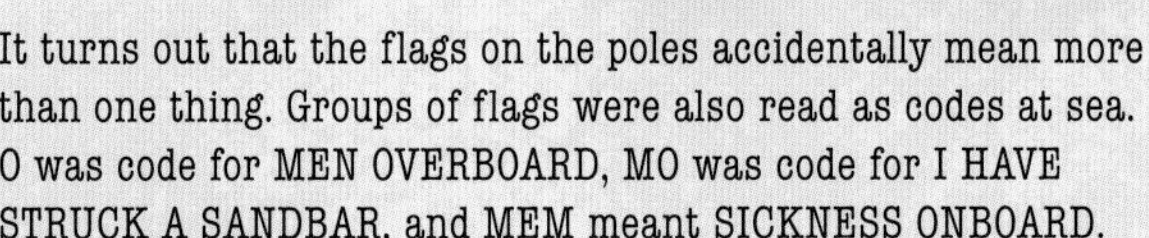

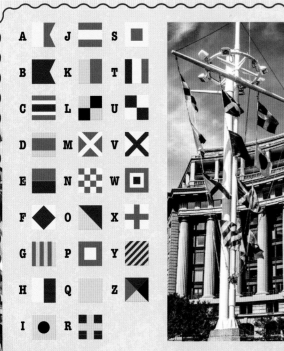

It turns out that the flags on the poles accidentally mean more than one thing. Groups of flags were also read as codes at sea. O was code for MEN OVERBOARD, MO was code for I HAVE STRUCK A SANDBAR, and MEM meant SICKNESS ONBOARD.

A WHEEL-Y GOOD VIEW

CAPITAL WHEEL

From the top of this giant Ferris wheel you can see the White House, the Washington Monument, and the Capitol, even though the wheel is 10 miles (16 km) away in Maryland. It has 1.6 million LED lights that are controlled by computer to create lots of different color displays to light up the Maryland sky.

"I can see my house from here!"
180 FT.
(54.8 M) HIGH

BRILLIANT BUILDINGS

There are some unique buildings and rooms around DC. Get ready to build your Washington knowledge and discover some surprises along this well-trodden trail through the city.

FIGHT!

THE PEACOCK ROOM, FREER GALLERY

This beautiful room is in the Smithsonian's Freer Gallery. It was brought over from London, where it was created in 1877 by artist James McNeill Whistler. He painted the room for a businessman named Frederick R. Leyland. When Whistler handed him a huge bill for the work ($200,000 in today's money), Leyland got angry and said he would only pay half! Whistler snuck back in and painted two fighting peacocks on the wall, with silver coins strewn on the ground around them, to represent himself and Leyland.

O STREET

MAGICAL MANSION

MANSION ON O STREET

This magical and weird hotel near Dupont Circle has over 60 hidden doors and secret passages. One of the passages can only be entered through a mirror! The hotel is also full of unusual treasures, including guitars signed by music legends such as Bruce Springsteen and Bob Dylan, and signed scripts for all three of *The Lord of the Rings* movies.

WATERMELON HOUSE

WHAT A WALL!

WATERMELON HOUSE

This unusually decorated home is a landmark in the Logan Circle neighborhood. The owners hired painters to paint their house red. The front turned out well, but the side looked more pink, which they didn't like. So they improvised and turned it into a giant mural of a watermelon.

search: DC STREET ART

Here are some other wondrous wall murals to be found around the city.

- **A wall of lovely hearts and a wall showing a giant blue eye at Union Market.**
- **A giant wave crashing over a boat in Georgetown.**
- **A steam train racing a classic car in Bethesda.**

THE END OF ABE

PETERSEN HOUSE

After he was shot at Ford's Theatre in 1865 (see page 47), doctors moved the unconscious Abraham Lincoln to a boarding house across the street, which was owned by William and Anna Petersen. Visitors can see the room where Lincoln died the next morning, aged 56. As the poor stricken president lay in bed, crowds gathered outside, and a stream of 90 VIPs were allowed in to pay their respects.

THE DYING LINCOLN WAS PUT IN A ROOM RENTED TO A UNION SOLDIER, WHO WAS AWAY AT THE TIME. WHEN THE SOLDIER RETURNED TO LIVE IN THE ROOM, HE COMPLAINED THAT TOURISTS KEPT COMING IN AND STEALING MEMENTOS.

PETERSEN HOUSE

BE A BUILDER

NATIONAL BUILDING MUSEUM

There are toolkits to use and lots of fun activities in this F Street museum all about building and design. Kids can build things themselves here and try their hand at being an interior designer or an engineer. Among its exhibits it has a collection of 2,300 building toys from different eras.

THE BUILDING MUSEUM IS THE HOME OF THE AMERICAN BRICK COLLECTION OF 1,500 BRICKS FROM AROUND THE COUNTRY. BUT HOW MANY BRICKS ARE IN THE WALLS OF THE MUSEUM ITSELF? SOMEBODY HAS COUNTED! TAKE A GUESS AND THEN LOOK AT THE ANSWER BELOW...

ANSWER: 15,500,000

NATIONAL BUILDING MUSEUM

ACACIA GRIFFINS

STONE MONSTER GUARDS

ACACIA GRIFFINS

These two giant stone griffins sit guarding the Acacia Building on Louisiana Avenue NW. There's a male on the right and a female on the left. They're each holding a nest of eggs between their paws, symbolizing how good they are at protecting their home. The building they guard was once owned by an insurance company.

GRIFFINS HAVE THE BODY OF A LION AND THE HEAD AND WINGS OF AN EAGLE.

ART OUTSIDE AND INSIDE

MURAL CHURCH

This building, built over 140 years ago, in 1875, used to be a church. It was left abandoned until artists took it over, wrapped an amazing mural around it, and opened an arts club for everyone near the Southwest Waterfront. The outside is bright with polka dots and patterns, and the inside is filled with murals, too.

IS IT A MAILBOX? NO, IT'S A MUSEUM!

HIRSHHORN MUSEUM

This modern art museum looks really different. The architect wanted it to look like a giant sculpture. Some people call it a concrete mailbox, and others think it looks like a drum. In the gardens outside, there are all sorts of unusual sculptures designed to get your imagination going.

WASHINGTON G-G-G-GHOSTS!

Perhaps it's not surprising that there are plenty of ghost stories in the capital. After all, why shouldn't spooks get in on all the fun? Don't worry, though. They won't bother you on this ghost-hunting trail. They're too busy appearing and disappearing!

STILL TRYING

M STREET BRIDGE

This bridge links the neighborhoods of Georgetown and Foggy Bottom. An earlier bridge on the site collapsed in a storm in 1788, and it's said that a stagecoach driver and his four horses drowned in the accident. The story goes that a ghostly stagecoach is sometimes seen trying to cross the bridge.

ACCORDING TO A SPOOKY STORY, THERE'S MORE THAN ONE GHOST ON THIS BRIDGE. SOME PEOPLE HAVE HEARD A YOUNG DRUMMER BOY, SAID TO HAVE FALLEN OFF THE BRIDGE BY ACCIDENT IN A HIGH WIND.

DON'T LOOK UP!

DECATUR HOUSE

Naval hero Stephen Decatur built this house on Lafayette Square in 1818. Fourteen months after moving in, he was wounded in a duel and died a few days later at home. Now, he's said to haunt the house, occasionally staring sadly out of the windows.

DECATUR HOUSE

GHOSTLY GUEST

HAY-ADAMS HOTEL

Lafayette Square is said to be DC's Ghost Central. There are several supposedly haunted spots around the square, including this hotel. Clover Adams – a socialite and much-admired photographer – is said to be an eternal guest here. She died in 1885, but it's said that she still occasionally wanders the halls whispering "What do you want?" Most people would probably reply "To run away from you!"

"Could I have a gin and tonic, please?"
"Sorry, we don't serve spirits"

HAY-ADAMS HOTEL

SPOOKY PEW

ST. JOHN'S CHURCH

St. John's Church is also a top spook spot on Lafayette Square. It is known as the Church of the Presidents because many presidents have attended services here. Pew 54 – the President's Pew – is reserved for the leader. The church bell is tolled when a president or ex-president dies, and that's when the spooks show up. It's been said that when the bell rings, six men in white robes appear in the President's Pew at midnight to pay their respects before fading away.

ST. JOHN'S CHURCH

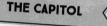

CUTTS-MADISON HOUSE

THE GHOST THAT ROCKS

CUTTS-MADISON HOUSE

This home is often called the Dolley Madison House. Dolley was the wife of James Madison (the fourth president of the US), and she lived here after his death. She is said to appear, rocking in her favorite chair, on the side of the house facing Lafayette Square (where a porch used to be). By all accounts, Dolley was a pleasant and popular first lady, so any surprised rocking-chair spotters shouldn't have anything to worry about.

PHANTOM FELINE

THE CAPITOL

Thanks to its long and dramatic history, the Capitol is said to be DC's most haunted building. The weirdest ghost prize has to be awarded to the Demon Cat (nicknamed so its initials are DC). He (or perhaps she) is said to be the ghost of a black cat that once patrolled the building catching rats. Now, the phantom feline roams the basement, leaving ghostly paw prints. Visitors can even see some tiny paw prints cast in concrete in one of the hallways.

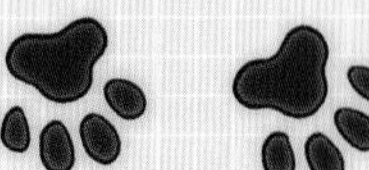

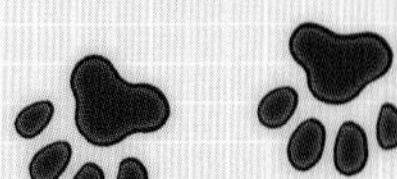

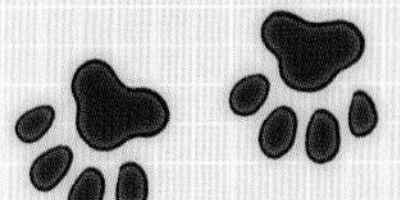

THE CAPITOL

Here are some of the spooks said to haunt the Capitol. It sounds crowded for the haunters on Capitol Hill!

- **A congressman who was shot on the stairs**
- **A slave who died building the Capitol**
- **A clerk who died when part of the building fell down**
- **A vice president who caught a chill in one of the Capitol's bathtubs and died of pneumonia**
- **Long-gone senators still giving speeches**
- **Ghostly librarians busy bustling around**
- **A Union soldier who died of his wounds in the building**

ROCK CREEK CEMETERY

STRANGE STATUE

ADAMS MEMORIAL, ROCK CREEK CEMETERY

This eerie-looking statue has a sad story attached to it. When writer Henry Adams's wife, Clover (the same Clover who haunts the Hay-Adams Hotel), killed herself in 1885, he was devastated. After a trip to Japan, he commissioned this memorial. It represents the Buddhist idea of nirvana, a state of peace and freedom from all feelings. The mysterious figure is neither male nor female, happy nor sad. It's a fascinating figure, just like the ghosts on this trail!

MARINE BARRACKS

GHOSTLY GOLD

MARINE BARRACKS

It is said that in August 1814, as British soldiers were approaching Washington and preparations were made to defend the city, two Marine sergeants were given the Marine Corps payroll (a chest full of gold coins) to guard. They buried it in the grounds of the barracks, but they were then killed, and the location of the treasure was lost. According to legend, their ghosts now wander the grounds, either looking for the lost chest of gold or guarding it. They're not saying!

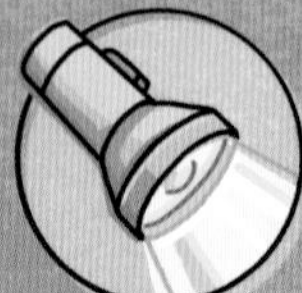

UNDERGROUND WASHINGTON

Follow the trail underground to discover some of the things hidden below the capital. There are tunnels, caverns, time capsules, and art, too.

ART UNDER THE STREET

DUPONT UNDERGROUND GALLERY

A huge abandoned trolley station lies underneath Dupont Circle. It covers a large area of underground platforms and tunnels that were all closed up in 1962. Now, it's been reopened and is used by artists, musical performers, and theater groups as a cool underground art space, just 8 ft. (2.4 m) below DC's busy streets.

HIDDEN CAVERNS

MCMILLAN SAND FILTRATION SITE

This northwest site was a water treatment plant until it was shut down in the 1980s. Its acres of eerie underground caverns used to be filled with sand, which was part of the filtration process. Ideas to redevelop the caverns include making an underground farm for growing vegetables under artificial light. Meanwhile, photographers have taken fantastic shots of the underground arches, looking like the vaults of an old cathedral or castle.

DUPONT CIRCLE

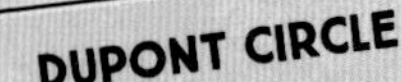

MCMILLAN SAND FILTRATION SITE

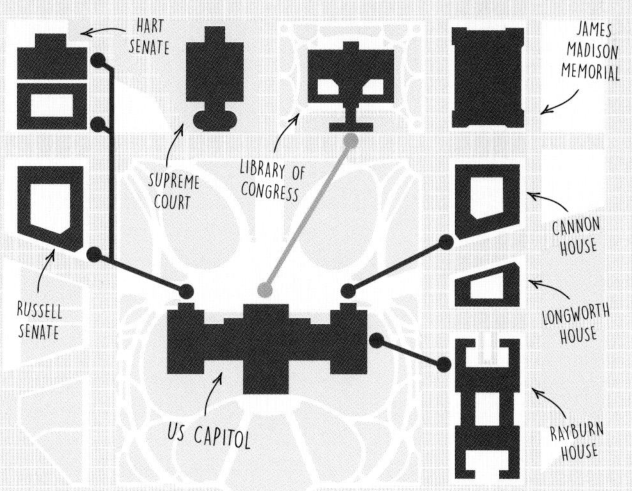

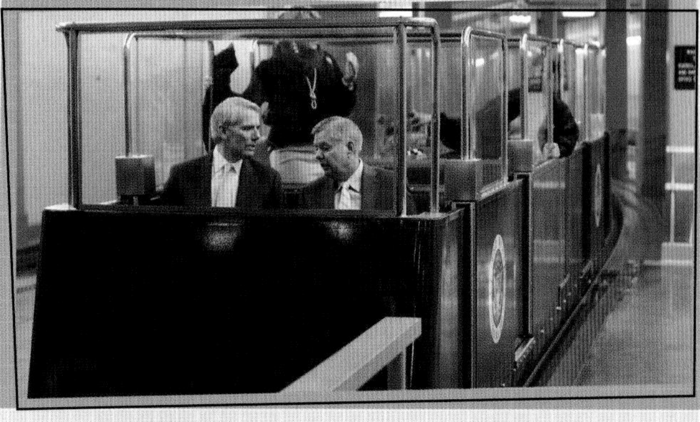

SENATE SHUTTLE

CAPITOL SUBWAY

One of the world's most exclusive (and shortest) subways runs between the House of Representatives and the Senate (the two parts of Congress). It's an electric people mover that's only used by members of Congress and invited guests. Journeys only take a minute or two but they save everyone having to trudge through the winter snows to vote.

TOP TUNNELS

LIBRARY OF CONGRESS TUNNELS

The Library of Congress and the Capitol buildings are connected by a system of tunnels. Tucked into the tunnels there are offices, a carpentry workshop, a masonry workshop, a cobbler, and even a donut shop!

IN THE CANNON TUNNEL, THE WALLS SHOWCASE ART FROM HIGH SCHOOL CHILDREN AROUND THE NATION. IT BRIGHTENS UP THE WALK FOR MEMBERS OF CONGRESS.

THE FIRST SUBWAY WAS ADDED IN 1909 AND CARRIED CONGRESSMEN VIA ELECTRIC CARS.

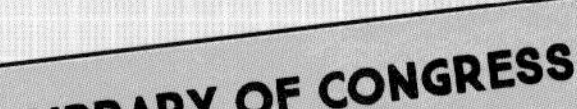

CAPITOL

TRUE OR FALSE?

TUNNEL UNDER THE MALL

There's a legend that the Smithsonian has an underground storage facility sprawling under the Mall, popularized by the movie *Night at the Museum: Battle of the Smithsonian*, but it's not true. The Smithsonian storage facilities are over in Suitland, Maryland (see page 83 to find out more). Sadly, there are no hidden secrets under the Mall, just a tunnel between the Smithsonian Castle and the National Museum of Natural History. It was built in 1909 for maintenance. It has the odd rat and roach, apparently, but no treasures.

SMITHSONIAN CASTLE

BELOW-GROUND BEAUTY

SMITHSONIAN UNDERGROUND MUSEUMS

The National Mall has loads of underground treasures, and they're on display for people to see. The Sackler Gallery of Asian Art, the National Museum of African Art, and the National Museum of African American History and Culture are 96 percent underground. The buildings are carefully designed to keep underground water out and let light in from above.

CRISIS LOCATION

WHITE HOUSE SITUATION ROOM

The "Sit Room," as it's known, is in the West Wing basement of the White House. It's a complex of rooms where the president and staff go to manage emergencies. It's staffed 24/7 to monitor national and international intelligence data. From here, the president can securely communicate with US military chiefs and heads of state around the world.

FREEDOM PLAZA

WHITE HOUSE

HIDDEN FOR HISTORY

TIME CAPSULE UNDER FREEDOM PLAZA

In 1988, Western Plaza became Freedom Plaza in memory of Martin Luther King Jr.'s famous "I Have a Dream" speech, given in 1963. A time capsule in his memory was buried underneath the plaza. When it is opened in 2088, historians will find MLK's Bible, a robe he wore to preach in, and recordings of some of his speeches.

search: TIME CAPSULES

There are many other time capsules hidden around the city, including these three:

- The cornerstone of the Supreme Court building hides a copy of the 1932 *World Almanac.*
- The cornerstone of the Jefferson Memorial hides a copy of the Declaration of Independence and the Constitution.
- President George W. Bush buried a time capsule in the White House gardens to celebrate its 200th anniversary. The capsule contains seeds from a magnolia tree, a flag, and a Christmas ornament, among other things.

RICH PICKINGS

By the time you've done this trail, you'll know exactly where to look for Washington's most valuable jewels, artifacts, and money piles. It's time for a treasure hunt!

NATIONAL CATHEDRAL

CONSTITUTIONAL COINS

FLOOR OF PENNIES, NATIONAL CATHEDRAL

The Lincoln Bay in the cathedral is named after the 16th president. It has 34 Lincoln pennies (one-cent coins engraved with Lincoln's head) embedded in the floor, in a star and circle shape. They represent the 34 US states at the time of Lincoln's inauguration. Legend has it that the central coin is placed face down to represent South Carolina, the first state to leave the Union at the beginning of the Civil War.

EGGS-TRAORDINARY!

FABERGÉ EGG, HILLWOOD MUSEUM

This museum was once the mansion of a wealthy heiress. She liked to collect Russian treasures, including the diamond-studded Catherine the Great Fabergé Egg created in 1914 for Russian royalty. It is made from engraved gold, with tiny enameled scenes, 937 diamonds, and 500 pearls. Only 40 Imperial Fabergé eggs are known to exist. The Hillwood has two of them, and owns nearly 90 Fabergé objects in all.

CATHERINE THE GREAT EGG

THE CATHERINE THE GREAT EGG ONCE HELD A TINY SURPRISE, NOW LOST. INSIDE THERE WAS A MECHANICAL LITTER CARRYING THE TINY FIGURE OF CATHERINE THE GREAT, EMPRESS OF RUSSIA IN THE 18TH CENTURY.

HILLWOOD MUSEUM

INDONESIAN EMBASSY

GONE GOLD

HIDDEN GOLD, INDONESIAN EMBASSY

The Indonesian Embassy, on Embassy Row, might have a secret hoard of lost gold! The gold-mining tycoon who originally built it in 1903 supposedly buried a gold nugget in the foundations and a gold bar in the archway above the front door. When the house became an embassy, its new owners searched for the gold but didn't find anything.

search: **WASHINGTON, DC, GOLD MINES**

- Back during the Civil War, there were tales of Union soldiers finding gold in streams just outside DC. In total, 45 gold mines were dug in the area, but none are still open.
- From time to time, there are reports of small amounts of gold found in streams, but if you're hoping to make your fortune, Washington probably isn't your best bet.

THE WORLD BANK

BANK OF BILLIONS

THE WORLD BANK

The World Bank is based on H Street but it's not the kind of bank where you would go to open an account. It aims to help get rid of extreme poverty around the world by lending billions of dollars to the governments of developing countries. It has a very unusual bank policy. It consults 12- to 18-year-olds around the world on the projects it funds in their countries. It says it wants to hear their views, not just the views of adults.

BLUE SPARKLER

HOPE DIAMOND

The biggest blue diamond in the world can be found at the National Museum of Natural History (also see page 25). During the French Revolution, when King Louis XVI and Marie Antoinette tried to escape from France, the diamond was turned over to the French government, but a year after that, it was stolen! It has reappeared and disappeared several times since then. In 1958, it was donated to the museum, where it still sits today, closely guarded and safe and sound... for now!

FAKE TAKE

US TREASURY

The Treasury Building has a burglar-proof vault that was once used to store millions of notes, coins, and gold bars. In 1905, a Berlin newspaper broke the story that the US government was hiding the fact that thieves had stolen $268 million from the building in a daring heist. Apparently, they had tunneled under the Potomac River to the building, loaded the money onto electric cars, and taken it back through the tunnel to small submarines. Other papers reprinted the story, but it turned out to be an April Fool's joke!

DC'S MOST VALUABLE

NATIONAL GALLERY OF ART

The most prized painting in the National Gallery is *Ginevra de' Benci*, painted in 1474 by Leonardo da Vinci. It's the only portrait by da Vinci in North America. The National Gallery bought the painting in February 1967 for around $5 million from Liechtenstein's royal family. It was then the most expensive art purchase known to the world.

55 MILLION
OBJECTS
OLDEST
4.6-BILLION-YEAR-OLD METEORITE

LEONARDO DA VINCI LEFT HIS FINGERPRINTS ON THE PAINTING WHEN HE USED HIS FINGER TO RUB SOME WET PAINT.

PART OF THE PORTRAIT MAY BE MISSING. THE SECTION WITH THE HANDS MAY HAVE BEEN CUT OFF IN THE PAST, TO MAKE THE PICTURE SMALLER.

SPARE STUFF

SMITHSONIAN STORAGE AREA

The Smithsonian has its own treasure hoard about 10 miles (16 km) southwest of Washington, in Suitland, Maryland. Here, it stores everything that isn't being shown in its museums – about 40 percent of what it owns. The collections are housed in five numbered buildings called pods, each about the size of a football field and three stories high. There are all kinds of things, from meteorites and poison blow darts to totem poles and dinosaur fossils. One, nicknamed the "wet pod," houses thousands of biological (animal) specimens preserved in liquid.

NATIONAL GALLERY OF ART

SMITHSONIAN STORAGE AREA

MAKING MONEY

US BUREAU OF ENGRAVING AND PRINTING

The bureau is the money factory of the US Federal Reserve. It prints about $560 million worth of new notes each day! New ones are needed because the average $1 bill lasts 5.8 years before it gets too tattered for general use.

THE MILLION-DOLLAR MUSEUM

Visitors to the bureau can see notes being printed and visit a museum all about money. They can stand next to a glass case filled with $1 million, stacked in $10 bills.

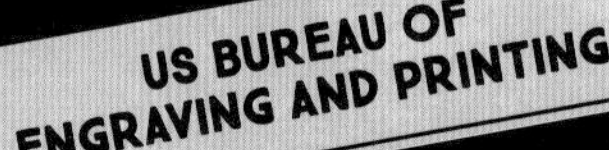

EARLY PRINTING

The first federal government paper money was issued in 1861. Before that, from 1793, US banks were allowed to create their own notes. There were even Christmas-themed notes with Santa on them. A rare Santa note sold for $40,000 in 2011.

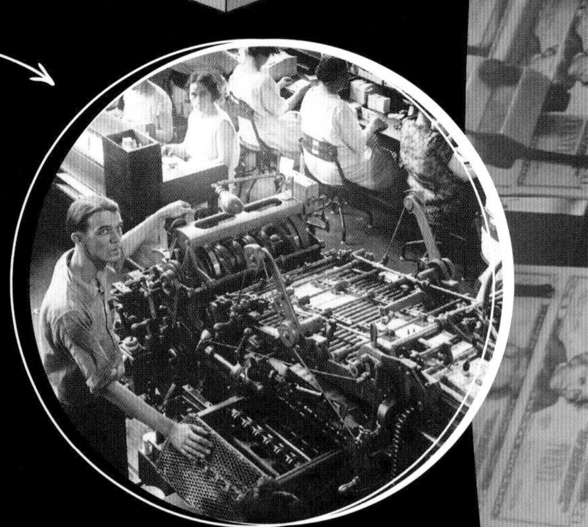

US MONEY IS ACTUALLY MADE OF FABRIC. IT'S PRINTED ON MATERIAL MADE OF 75 PERCENT COTTON AND 25 PERCENT LINEN.

BIGGEST EVER

The highest-value bank note now printed is the $100 bill. There have been higher notes, but these are no longer made. If you find one, you can still use it, or perhaps sell it to a collector of rare money. In 1934 and 1935, the bureau printed $100,000 bills, for just three weeks.

24.8 MILLION

NUMBER OF NOTES PRINTED EACH DAY

$1.43 TRILLION

APPROXIMATE VALUE OF ALL THE US NOTES IN CIRCULATION AT ANY ONE TIME

HOW TO MAKE A DOLLAR

1. FIRST, DESIGNERS CREATE COMPLICATED DESIGNS THAT ARE HARD TO FAKE.
2. ENGRAVERS TRANSFER THE DESIGNS TO STEEL DIES, WITH ALL THE FINE LINES AND GROOVES NEEDED TO PRINT THE PICTURE.
3. PRINTING MACHINES ADD BACKGROUND COLOR.
4. GREEN AND BLACK INK ARE ADDED, ALONG WITH SEALS.
5. NOTES GET THEIR SERIAL NUMBERS AND ARE INSPECTED USING COMPUTER TECHNOLOGY BEFORE BEING SEPARATED.

US notes were redesigned in the 2000s to make it harder to make fake money. Here are some of the features now built in to different notes:

- **A security thread that glows under ultraviolet light and has its own letters and numbers**
- **Raised areas of printing you can feel with your finger**
- **A portrait that appears when you hold a note up to the light**
- **Ink that changes color when you tilt the note**

WATER WORLD

Put on your boots and come splashing along Washington's watery trail. Look out for sinking ponds, magical sea creatures, presidential baths, sewage power, and one very embarrassed swimmer along the way!

NATION'S RIVER

POTOMAC RIVER

The Potomac is nicknamed the "Nation's River." It used to be very polluted and smelly, but it's been cleaned up in recent years. Swimming isn't allowed these days, but John Quincy Adams (the sixth president) used to swim in it naked every day, early in the morning. A journalist called Anne Royall once caught him swimming, stood on his clothes on the shore, and forced him to give her an interview in the water before she agreed to go away!

WORKING WATERWAY

C & O CANAL

The Chesapeake & Ohio Canal starts in Georgetown and stretches to Cumberland in Maryland. It was built in the first half of the 19th century to carry coal from the Allegheny Mountains. Mules pulled the boats along from the towpaths by the side of the canal. The mules lived on the boats, along with boat families. The front cabin was usually made into a stable.

POTOMAC RIVER

90%

OF DC'S DRINKING WATER COMES FROM THE POTOMAC RIVER

383 MILES (616 KM) LONG

The Potomac River runs through West Virginia, Virginia, Maryland, Pennsylvania, and DC.

WATER IN THE WHITE HOUSE

WHITE HOUSE

These days, the White House has an incredible 35 bathrooms, but back when it was first built, there was no water supply at all. Servants had to lug buckets of water from a spring five blocks away. There was no running water until 1833, so any presidents before that time would have had their baths in portable bathtubs filled by buckets. No wonder John Quincy Adams swam in the river every morning!

WHITE HOUSE

LINCOLN MEMORIAL

POOL FOR PRESIDENTS

REFLECTING POOL

The Reflecting Pool runs between the Lincoln Memorial and the Washington Monument. It is based on pools in the gardens of French royal palaces. First built in 1920 on marshland, it soon began to sink and leak, so it had to be reconstructed. Its peaceful surface hides a noisy secret. The busy Interstate 395 runs through a tunnel right underneath it!

BIOENERGY FACILITY

WATERPOWER

BIOENERGY FACILITY

The city does not waste its waste! DC Water turns used water and poop into power at the Blue Plains Advanced Wastewater Treatment Plant, in the city's southwest sector. Here's how:

Water and sewage from DC's sinks, showers, and toilets travel to the plant, where the solids are separated from the liquids, which then flow to a water treatment plant.

The solids are heated, sterilized, and sent to a digester, where microbes eat them. This produces methane gas, which is burned to generate electricity.

The solid material that's left is completely clean and makes great farm compost.

370 MILLION GALLONS

(1,682 MILLION LITERS)

DC Water treats enough sewage daily to fill Washington's RFK Stadium.

NAVAL LAND BASE

NAVY YARD

The Navy Yard has been in operation for over 200 years, and it was the US Navy's first-ever shore site. Today, it's the home of the chief of naval operations of the US Navy, a VIP four-star admiral. At the National Museum of the US Navy in the yard, there are all kinds of historic sea-based artifacts, including the inside of a submarine with working periscopes.

THERE'S A 20-MILE (32 KM) WALK ALONG THE ANACOSTIA RIVER BY THE NAVY YARD, AND IN THE YARD'S PARK, THERE'S A POOL AND WATERFALL FOR EVERYONE TO SPLASH IN. IT'S A GREAT PLACE TO COOL DOWN IN SUMMER.

NAVY YARD

THE OCEAN COMES TO DC

BARTHOLDI FOUNTAIN

This lovely fountain, set in its own park, looks beautiful when it is lit up at night. It's made of cast iron and it represents light and water. It's decorated with chubby little tritons (sea gods) playing with seaweed and three sea nymphs standing on tiptoe among shells and coral. At the bottom, turtles spray jets of water from their mouths.

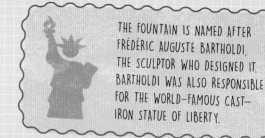

THE FOUNTAIN IS NAMED AFTER FRÉDÉRIC AUGUSTE BARTHOLDI, THE SCULPTOR WHO DESIGNED IT. BARTHOLDI WAS ALSO RESPONSIBLE FOR THE WORLD-FAMOUS CAST-IRON STATUE OF LIBERTY.

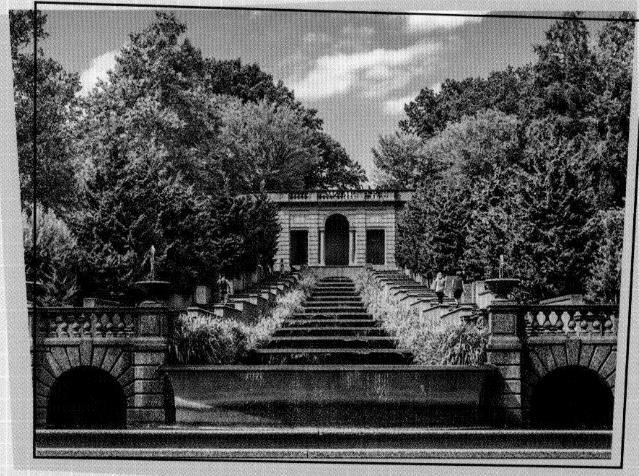

NATION'S LONGEST

MERIDIAN HILL PARK FOUNTAIN

The design of this DC park was based on Italian gardens of the past, and it has the longest cascading fountain in the US. The water is pumped around and around, between 13 different basins. Years before the park was built on the hill, the area was a campsite for Union soldiers during the Civil War.

MERIDIAN HILL PARK FOUNTAIN

GO WASHINGTON

Climb aboard for a transportation trail that will take you all around town. Hitch a ride with the president, take a foreign flight, or travel on the Metro. Look for Ancient Romans, horses, and alligators on your journey...

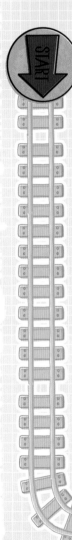

GATEWAY TO THE WORLD

DULLES AIRPORT

Famed architect Eero Saarinen designed this airport with swooping shapes and giant windows to evoke the feeling of flight, as if the building itself is getting ready for takeoff! Most of Washington's international flights arrive and depart from here, although it's in Virginia, a few miles outside the city. The airport's busiest international route is to and from London Heathrow in the UK.

CHILDREN CAN TAKE TOURS OF THE AIRPORT TO LEARN ALL ABOUT ITS BEHIND-THE-SCENES WORK. THEY CAN MEET THE CLEVER EXPLOSIVES-HUNTING DOGS OF THE AIRPORT'S K-9 DETECTION UNIT, WHO HELP WITH AIRPORT SECURITY.

PRESIDENTS DON'T DO TRAFFIC JAMS!

MARINE ONE

The president's helicopter is operated by Marine Helicopter Squadron One (HMX-1), who are nicknamed the "Nighthawks." They're based at the Marine Corps Air Facility in Quantico, Virginia, 40 miles (64 km) from the White House. The helicopter lands on the White House south lawn when it comes to pick up or drop off the president, avoiding DC's traffic jams.

DULLES AIRPORT

WHITE HOUSE

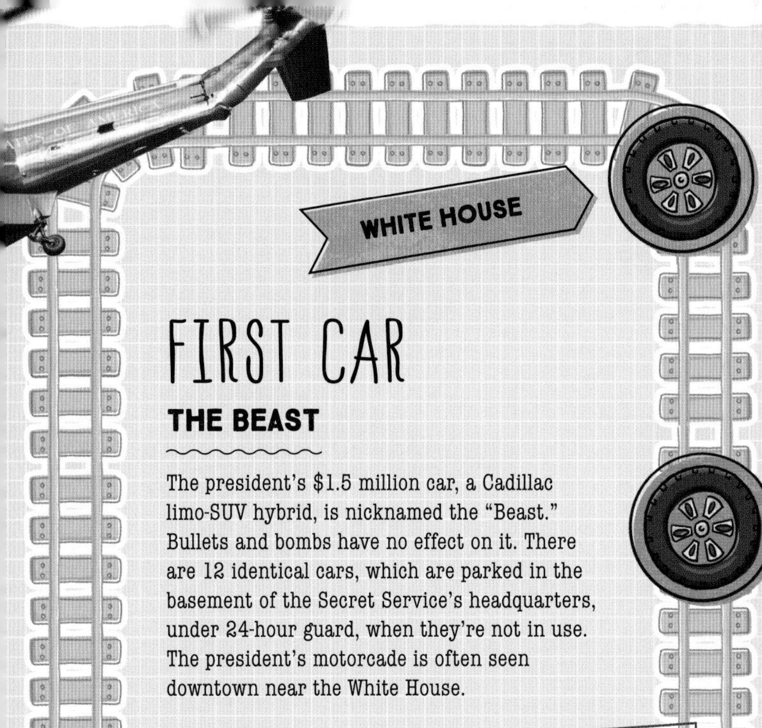

FIRST CAR

THE BEAST

The president's $1.5 million car, a Cadillac limo-SUV hybrid, is nicknamed the "Beast." Bullets and bombs have no effect on it. There are 12 identical cars, which are parked in the basement of the Secret Service's headquarters, under 24-hour guard, when they're not in use. The president's motorcade is often seen downtown near the White House.

8 IN.
(20 CM)
THICKNESS OF ARMORED CAR DOORS

THE TIRES ARE PUNCTURE-RESISTANT, BUT THE CAR COULD RUN ON ITS STEEL RIMS IF THEY BLEW!

THERE IS USUALLY A DECOY CAR IN THE MOTORCADE, WITH A PRESIDENTIAL LOOK-ALIKE INSIDE.

REAGAN NATIONAL AIRPORT

FLYING OVER THE PAST

REAGAN NATIONAL AIRPORT

In Terminal A there's a reminder of Washington's past. Before the airport was built here, across the river from downtown DC, Native American people lived on the site. Later, it was a plantation owned by George Washington's stepson. Travelers in Terminal A can see artifacts found by archaeologists, which reveal the airport's surprising past secrets, including pottery made and used by the slaves who would have once worked on the plantation.

ARRIVE IN STYLE

UNION STATION

Trains traveling around the country leave from and arrive in this grand old station. It was first opened in 1908, and it was then the largest station in the world. It's been renovated with $160 million to look as beautiful as it once did. Here are some unusual facts about it that you can use to surprise your friends if you ever visit!

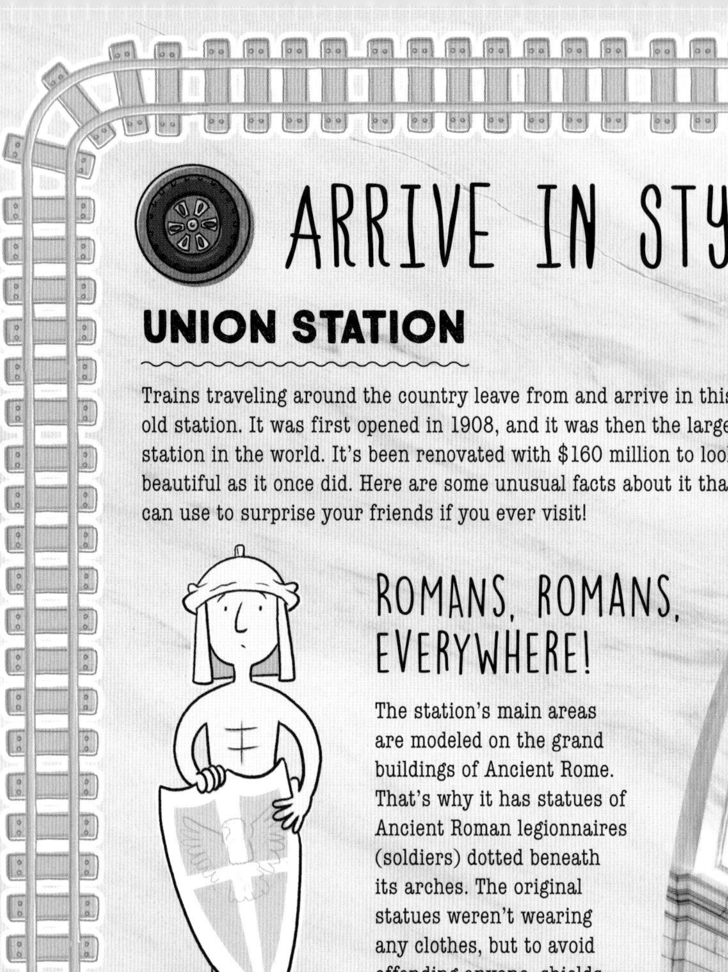

ROMANS, ROMANS, EVERYWHERE!

The station's main areas are modeled on the grand buildings of Ancient Rome. That's why it has statues of Ancient Roman legionnaires (soldiers) dotted beneath its arches. The original statues weren't wearing any clothes, but to avoid offending anyone, shields were added to cover them up.

THE PUZZLE OF THE CLOCK

The large clock in the station's Main Hall is 6 ft. (1.8 m) wide. It has Roman numerals marked on it, but the Roman numeral for number 4 is IV, and the clock is marked IIII. Nobody knows why some clocks have been marked in this way for centuries. It's one of history's mysteries!

22-CARAT GOLD LEAF
THE CEILING OF THE GRAND CONCOURSE IS BARREL-VAULTED (MADE INTO A LONG ARCH) AND COFFERED (IT HAS LOTS OF SUNKEN PANELS).
ANCIENT ROMAN LEGIONNAIRES

VIPS WELCOME

THE STATION HAD LUXURY FACILITIES FOR ITS MOST IMPORTANT PASSENGERS. PRESIDENTS, KINGS, AND QUEENS ALL PASSED THROUGH THE STATION, AND THERE WAS A PRESIDENTIAL SUITE FOR WELCOMING VIPS. IT WAS SHAPED LIKE THE WHITE HOUSE OVAL OFFICE.

90,000+
NUMBER OF DAILY VISITORS

32 MILLION+
NUMBER OF VISITORS YEARLY

SMELLY OUTSIDE

When the station was first built, it was next to a shanty town neighborhood called Swampoodle, on the banks of a stinky, sewage-filled creek.

GODS OF THE STATION

There are six statues at the entrance to the station that look like they come from Ancient Greece:

Prometheus – In Greek mythology, he gave fire to humans

Thales – A Greek math and science genius who was the first person ever to study electricity

Themis – Goddess of law and justice

Apollo – God of knowledge

Ceres – Goddess of agriculture

Archimedes – A brilliant mathematician and inventor

RETURN OF RETRO TRAVEL

STREETCARS

In the early 20th century, the streets of DC were crammed with streetcars. Then, buses came into fashion, and streetcars stopped running. Now they're back, starting with the H Street streetcar, which starts its route at Union Station. Streetcars run on tracks and are powered by electricity from substations along the line, making them much better for the environment than buses.

RIDING ROUND TOWN

METRO

DC's subway and bus system is called the Metro. The subway covers around 118 miles (190 km), and it's the second-busiest rail system in the US, after New York. In 2006, Virginian Randi Miller won a nationwide contest to be the voice of the subway. Her voice tells everyone that the doors are opening or closing. The Metro's Wheaton Station has the longest escalator in the western hemisphere. It's the length of two football fields.

METRO

THE FIRST WASHINGTON STREETCARS WERE PULLED ALONG BY HORSES.

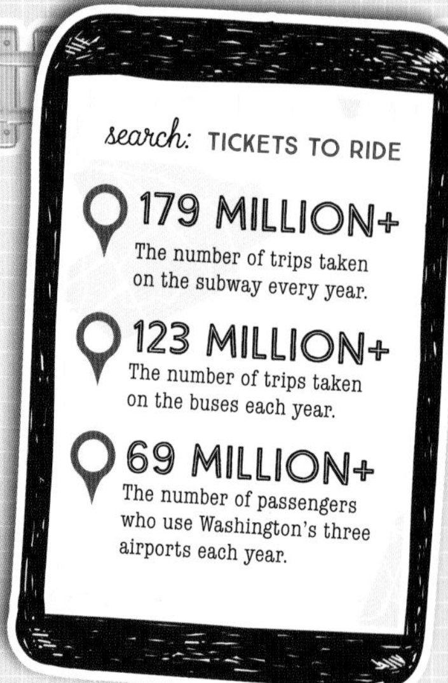

search: TICKETS TO RIDE

179 MILLION+
The number of trips taken on the subway every year.

123 MILLION+
The number of trips taken on the buses each year.

69 MILLION+
The number of passengers who use Washington's three airports each year.

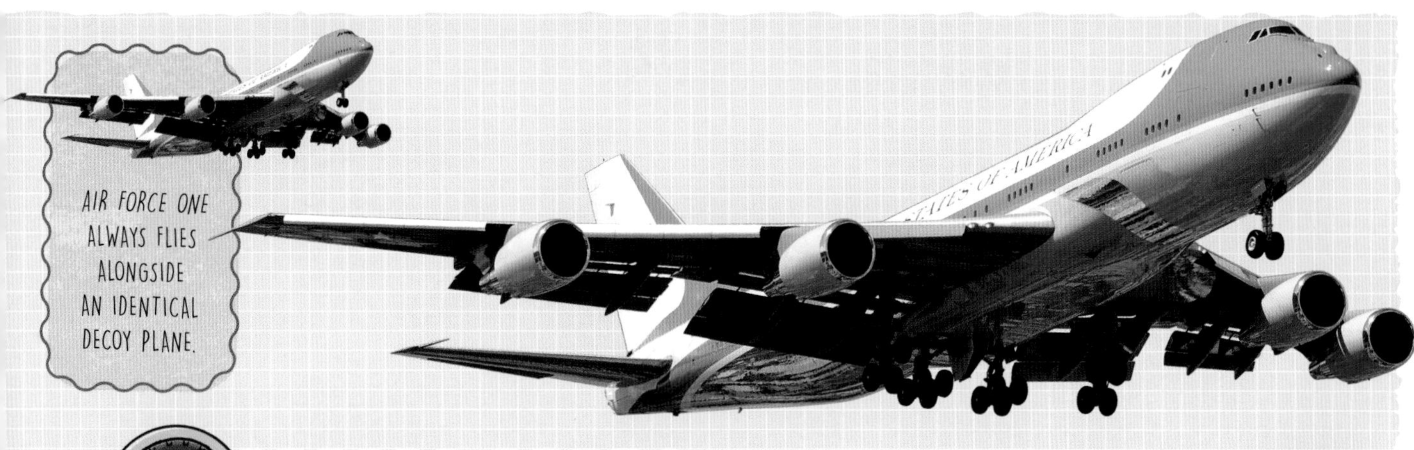

AIR FORCE ONE ALWAYS FLIES ALONGSIDE AN IDENTICAL DECOY PLANE.

LOST AND FOUND OFFICE

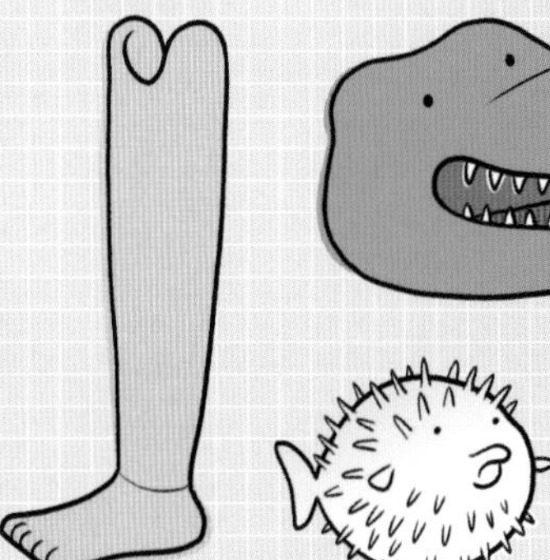

LOST A LEG? HOP ALONG HERE!

METRO LOST AND FOUND

AROUND 300 CELL PHONES ARE LOST ON THE METRO EACH MONTH.

The Metro's Lost and Found Office is in Hyattsville, Maryland, just over the DC border. Approximately 1,500 objects are handed in each month. Cell phones and wallets are the most-lost items, but Metro workers have found all kinds of strange items left behind by passengers. Weird examples include dead specimens of sea creatures, a prosthetic leg, and a stuffed alligator head!

AIR FORCE ONE

THE PRESIDENT'S PLANE

AIR FORCE ONE

The president's plane parks at Joint Base Andrews in Maryland, a few miles from the White House. It can travel any distance because it can refuel in the air. It has the latest defense systems and communications equipment on board. There is a suite of rooms for the president and staff, and kitchens big enough to make meals for 100 people. There's even an onboard operating room and a doctor.

SHOWTIME!

Pull back the curtains. Strike up the music. It's time for a DC show! There's plenty of song and dance, acting, and music around the city.

LINCOLN MEMORIAL STEPS

DECORATED BY THE WORLD

KENNEDY CENTER

Welcome to the city's top performing arts hall, and possibly the busiest arts venue in the whole of the US! Music of all kinds, ballet, and theater are all on the bill. Built as a memorial to assassinated President John F. Kennedy, more than 60 nations donated gifts to help decorate it, including beautiful art, sculpture, and lighting.

KENNEDY CENTER

START

SONGS ON THE STEPS

LINCOLN MEMORIAL STEPS

A historic concert occurred on the memorial steps on April 9, 1939, when singer Marian Anderson performed to a crowd of 75,000 people and a radio audience of millions. Constitution Hall was the largest venue in DC at the time, but the owners refused to allow Anderson to perform there because she was black. President Roosevelt and his wife, Eleanor, disagreed with the discrimination, so they invited Marian to hold her concert at the Lincoln Memorial instead. It was a nationwide success.

MUSIC ON THE MALL

SMITHSONIAN FOLKLIFE FESTIVAL

What do different parts of the world sound and taste like? Every summer, more than a million people find out by going to the Mall for free folk music, dance, crafts, storytelling, and food. The fun focuses on one or two countries each year. There are homegrown performers, too, showcasing music from different parts of the US.

THE DRUM MAJOR OF THE OLD GUARD FIFE AND DRUM CORPS CARRIES AN ESPONTOON. SEE IF ANYONE YOU KNOW CAN GUESS WHAT THAT IS BEFORE YOU TELL THEM! IT'S A KIND OF PIKE WEAPON – A POLE WITH A POINTED METAL BLADE ON THE END.

STRIKE UP THE BANDS

DC MILITARY MUSIC

Since 1863, the Army, Navy, Marine Corps, and Air Force bands have performed throughout the summer on the Capitol's West Front steps. Meanwhile, at Fort Myer in Arlington, visitors might see the Old Guard Fife and Drum Corps, men and women who dress and play as General George Washington's army musicians did in the 1700s. They wear tricorn (three-cornered) hats, white wigs, and red coats.

NATIONAL THEATRE

FRIENDLY STAGE SPOOK

NATIONAL THEATRE

This venue is nicknamed the "Theatre of Presidents" because it's near the White House. The friendly ghost of 19th-century actor John McCullough is said to haunt the place, after he was shot and killed by a fellow performer. McCullough's spirit is said to roam on the eve of opening nights. In 1982, a rusty old pistol was unearthed under the stage. It could have been the murder weapon, but we'll never know.

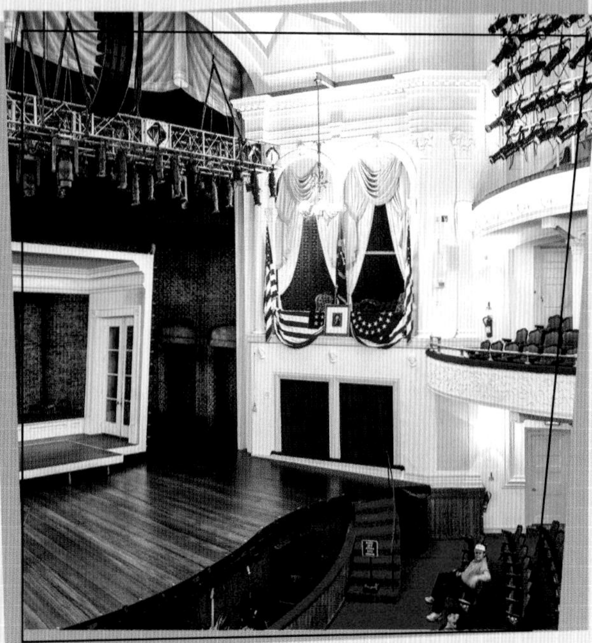

AT THE LOUDEST LAUGH

FORD'S THEATRE

When John Wilkes Booth assassinated Abraham Lincoln in his box seat here (see page 47), the doomed president was watching a comic play called *Our American Cousin*. Booth knew the play and exactly when the audience would laugh the most. He shot Lincoln at that very moment to muffle the sound.

LINCOLN HAD SEEN HIS ASSASSIN, JOHN WILKES BOOTH, BEFORE IN THE THEATER. HE ONCE WATCHED WILKES BOOTH PLAY THE TITLE ROLE IN SHAKESPEARE'S *RICHARD III*, AT THE NATIONAL THEATRE.

FORD'S THEATRE

OUT IN THE WOODS

CHILDREN'S THEATRE-IN-THE-WOODS

Out in Virginia, a few miles from downtown DC, there's a path and a bridge that lead to a magical circle of trees in a wood. This peaceful spot is called Wolf Trap. It's the home of the Children's Theatre, where local kids come to see music, dancing, puppets, and storytellers throughout the summer.

search: DC ON SCREEN

Washington has featured in many movies over the years, and the best of them have been nominated for, or even won, Academy Awards, including:

- **ALL THE PRESIDENT'S MEN**
- **FORREST GUMP**
- **JFK**
- **MR. SMITH GOES TO WASHINGTON**

HOME OF THE DUKE

BLACK BROADWAY

U Street NW was once known as Black Broadway. Many black musicians performed here in the first half of the 20th century – due to segregation, they had no choice but to perform in their own venues. Famous jazz maestro Duke Ellington was born on U Street. He went on to lead one of the best jazz swing bands in the world. Make sure you check out his big hit "Take the A Train"! His statue stands in front of the local Howard Theatre, still playing up a storm on the piano keys.

INDEX

INDEX

FURTHER READING

The Cities Book
Lonely Planet Kids

This book introduces you to lots of cities, including Washington. Find out fun facts on culture, history, and day-to-day life in the US capital, and compare DC with other cities around the world.

The Kid's Guide to Washington, DC
by Eileen Ogintz

Get travel tips from kids for visiting DC. Packed with facts, games, and quizzes, use this book to plan a family-friendly trip to Washington.

Mission Washington, D.C.: A Scavenger Hunt Adventure
by Catherine Aragon

This book is full of fun activities for kids to complete on trips around DC. Go on your own mission, and see if you can earn enough points to become a special agent

Who Was Martin Luther King, Jr.?
by Bonnie Bader

Find out more about the famous civil rights activist, who peacefully campaigned against discrimination based on race. Ideal for school projects.

Curious About the White House
by Kate Waters

Perfect for younger readers. You can step inside one of the most famous buildings in the world with this book and discover some of its secrets.

North American Indian
Dorling Kindersley Eyewitness

Uncover the stories of the first nations of North America. This book covers a range of different groups of people and will give kids a great insight into the cultural history of the US.